Preface

Welcome to the **macOS Interview Questions and Answers Book**, a powerful and user-friendly operating system that has captured the hearts of millions around the globe. This book, "mac OS Interview Questions & Answers," is designed to be your comprehensive guide to navigating the intricacies of this operating system, whether you are a seasoned professional or a curious enthusiast.

In today's rapidly evolving tech landscape, possessing a solid understanding of mac OS is essential for anyone looking to excel in the field of information technology. This book aims to provide you with a deep dive into the key concepts, features, and challenges associated with mac OS, ensuring that you are well-prepared for any interview scenario.

As you embark on this journey, it's important to note that this book is not just a collection of questions and answers. While it does include a range of thought-provoking queries commonly asked in interviews, the primary focus is on fostering a holistic understanding of mac OS. We believe that true mastery of a subject comes from a combination of theoretical knowledge and practical application.

The structure of this book is designed to facilitate a progressive learning experience. We begin with foundational concepts, ensuring that even those new to mac OS can build a solid base. From there, we delve into more advanced topics, covering a broad spectrum of subjects such as system architecture, file management, security protocols, and troubleshooting techniques. Each section is accompanied by a set of carefully curated interview questions and detailed answers to help you reinforce your understanding.

It's important to recognize that the world of technology is dynamic and ever-changing. As such, this book encourages you to approach mac OS with a mindset of continuous learning. Beyond the scope of interview preparation, the insights gained from this book can be applied to real-world scenarios, making you a more confident and effective user or administrator of mac systems.

Table of Contents

Chapter 1: Introduction to mac OS

Overview of mac OS

1 .What is the core philosophy behind mac OS design?

Answer:mac OS follows the principle of simplicity, user-friendly interfaces, and seamless integration of hardware and software.

2. Explain the role of Finder in mac OS.

Answer: Finder is the file management application that allows users to browse files, manage documents, and organize their system on mac OS.

3.How does Time Machine work, and why is it important for mac OS users?

Answer: Time Machine is a backup feature that automatically backs up the entire system. It's crucial for data recovery and system restoration in case of failures.

4. Describe the key features of mac OS Dock.

Answer: The Dock provides quick access to applications, documents, and features. It includes the Trash, frequently used apps, and system preferences.

5. What is Spotlight Search, and how does it enhance user productivity?

Answer: Spotlight is a search feature that allows users to find files, launch applications, and perform calculations quickly, enhancing overall system navigation.

6. Explain the concept of Gatekeeper in mac OS.

Answer: Gatekeeper is a security feature that ensures only trusted software is installed on a Mac, providing a layer of protection against malware.

7. How does FileVault contribute to mac OS security, and what are its benefits?

Answer: FileVault is disk encryption that secures data on the startup disk. It protects sensitive information, ensuring confidentiality and integrity.

8. Describe the role of Terminal in mac OS and its significance for advanced users.

Answer: Terminal is a command-line interface for mac OS, providing advanced users with direct access to the Unix-based system for scripting and customization.

9. What is iCloud, and how does it integrate with mac OS?

Answer: iCloud is Apple's cloud service. It integrates with mac OS, allowing seamless synchronization of data, such as photos, documents, and settings, across devices.

10. How can you troubleshoot common network connectivity issues on mac OS?

Answer: Troubleshooting may involve checking network settings, renewing DHCP leases, resetting Wi-Fi configurations, and examining system logs for clues.

11. Explain the role of Launchpad in mac OS and its relationship with the App Store.

Answer: Launchpad provides a visual representation of installed applications, akin to iOS. It complements the App Store for app management and installations.

12. Discuss the significance of system logs in mac OS for system administrators.

Answer: System logs, available in the Console app, provide detailed information on system events, errors, and processes, aiding in troubleshooting and monitoring.

13. How does mac OS manage hardware resources, and what are the tools available for performance tuning?

Answer:mac OS utilizes technologies like Grand Central Dispatch and Instruments for efficient resource management. Tools like Activity Monitor assist in performance tuning.

14. Describe the steps involved in configuring Time Machine for network backups.

Answer: Configuring Time Machine for network backups involves selecting a network drive, ensuring proper permissions, and configuring backup intervals in System Preferences.

15. Can you explain the role of Terminal profiles in customization and improving productivity?

Answer: Terminal profiles allow users to customize the appearance and behavior of the Terminal, providing a personalized and efficient command-line experience.

Evolution of mac OS

General Mac OS Evolution Questions:

1. Can you provide an overview of the major milestones in the evolution of mac OS over the past 15 years?

Answer: Certainly. Mac OS has undergone significant changes, including transitions from PowerPC to Intel architecture, the introduction of Mac OS X, and subsequent mac OS releases with advancements in performance, design, and features.

2. How has the user interface of Mac OS evolved over the years, and what impact has it had on user experience?

Answer: The user interface has evolved from Aqua in Mac OS X to the modern flat design in recent mac OS versions. These changes aim to enhance user experience, providing a more intuitive and visually appealing interface.

3. Can you discuss the transition from mac OS versions using big cat names (e.g., Snow Leopard) to mac OS versions named after California landmarks (e.g., Yosemite)?

Answer: The transition was symbolic, representing a shift from a focus on internal improvements to external features and enhancements. It also aligned with Apple's California-centric approach to product naming.

4. How has Apple's integration of iOS features into mac OS, such as iCloud and continuity, influenced the evolution of the operating system?

Answer: The integration has led to a seamless user experience across Apple devices. Features like Handoff and iCloud Drive enhance productivity and create a unified ecosystem for users.

Technical Questions:

1. Explain the significance of the transition from PowerPC to Intel processors in the evolution of Mac OS.

Answer: The transition to Intel processors in 2006 marked a major shift, allowing for increased performance, better power efficiency, and the ability to run Windows applications through Boot Camp.

2. Discuss the role of the UNIX-based foundation in mac OS and how it contributes to the stability and security of the operating system.

Answer: The UNIX foundation provides a robust and secure platform. It supports features like Terminal, and the permission system enhances security by restricting access to critical system files.

3. How has the evolution of Mac OS contributed to advancements in graphics and multimedia capabilities, especially considering the introduction of Metal?

Answer: Metal, introduced in mac OS El Capitan, significantly improved graphics performance by providing lower-level access to the GPU. This has benefited gaming, video editing, and other graphics-intensive applications.

4. Explain the significance of the transition to Apple Silicon, and how it has impacted the performance and efficiency of Mac computers.

Answer: The transition to Apple Silicon, starting with M1, marked a shift to custom-designed ARM-based processors. This has resulted in significant performance gains, improved energy efficiency, and a unified architecture across Apple's product line.

Software Development and Integration:

1. How has the evolution of Xcode and developer tools influenced the mac OS development ecosystem?

Answer: Xcode improvements, including enhanced debugging tools and interface builders, have streamlined the development process. Swift, introduced in 2014, has become a powerful language for mac OS development.

2. Discuss the impact of the Mac App Store on software distribution and the mac OS application ecosystem.

Answer: The Mac App Store has provided a centralized platform for software distribution, making it easier for users to discover and install applications. However, it has also faced challenges with app discoverability.

3. How has the introduction of Catalyst affected the development of cross-platform applications for both mac OS and iOS?

Answer: Catalyst allows developers to create apps that run on both mac OS and iOS with a shared codebase. It streamlines development and encourages consistency in user experience across different devices.

Security and Privacy:

1. Discuss the evolution of security features in mac OS, including technologies like Gatekeeper and FileVault.

Answer: Gatekeeper ensures only trusted software runs on a Mac, while FileVault provides full-disk encryption. These features, along with regular security updates, contribute to mac OS's reputation for strong security.

2. How has Apple addressed user privacy concerns in recent mac OS updates, such as App Tracking Transparency and Privacy Labels in the App Store?

Answer: Apple has taken a proactive approach to user privacy by introducing features like App Tracking Transparency, giving users more control over their data. Privacy Labels in the App Store provide transparency about how apps handle user data.

User Experience and Design:

1. Discuss the role of Dark Mode in recent mac OS versions and its impact on user experience.

Answer: Dark Mode provides users with an alternative visual style, reducing eye strain in low-light environments. It's a design choice that enhances user comfort and personalization.

2. How has the evolution of Mac OS contributed to accessibility features, such as VoiceOver and Dynamic Type, and their impact on inclusivity?

Answer: Accessibility features have been integral to mac OS, making the operating system usable by individuals with different abilities. VoiceOver and Dynamic Type are examples of features that enhance inclusivity.

Productivity and Collaboration:

1. Discuss the integration of collaboration features like Continuity Camera and Handoff and their impact on user productivity across Apple devices.

Answer: These features seamlessly connect Macs, iPhones, and iPads, allowing users to start an activity on one device and continue on another. It enhances productivity and provides a cohesive user experience.

2. How has the evolution of mac OS contributed to advancements in virtual collaboration tools, especially in response to changing work trends?

Answer:mac OS has adapted to the increasing demand for virtual collaboration tools, integrating with popular platforms and optimizing performance for remote work scenarios.

System Performance and Optimization:

1. Explain how technologies like Core Animation and Grand Central Dispatch contribute to system performance in mac OS.

Answer: Core Animation facilitates smooth animations, while Grand Central Dispatch optimizes the use of multicore processors, improving overall system performance.

2. Discuss the role of system optimization techniques like memory compression and App Nap in enhancing the overall performance and efficiency of mac OS.

Answer: Memory compression reduces the pressure on physical memory, while App Nap conserves resources for apps in the background, collectively contributing to a more efficient and responsive system.

Networking and Connectivity:

1. How has the evolution of mac OS addressed networking challenges, and what improvements have been made in terms of Wi-Fi technology and connectivity?

Answer:mac OS updates have included enhancements to Wi-Fi performance, security, and connectivity. Features like Wi-Fi Assist prioritize stable connections and mitigate network issues.

2. Discuss the role of Continuity features in mac OS, such as Handoff and Universal Clipboard, in providing a seamless experience across Apple devices.

Answer: Continuity features enable a smooth transition between devices, allowing users to start an activity on one device and seamlessly continue on another. This integration enhances the overall user experience.

Future Developments:

1. What are your expectations for the future evolution of mac OS, considering recent trends and technological advancements?

Answer:I anticipate further integration with Apple's ecosystem, advancements in machine learning applications, and continued improvements in performance and security.

2. How might the ongoing transition to Apple Silicon influence the development and capabilities of mac OS in the coming years?

Answer: The transition to Apple Silicon will likely result in increased performance, energy efficiency, and a more unified experience across Apple devices, as seen with recent M1-powered Macs.

Troubleshooting and Support:

1. Can you share experiences where you've had to troubleshoot complex issues on mac OS, and how you approached problem-solving?

Answer: Certainly. In a previous role, I encountered issues with software compatibility after a mac OS update. I systematically identified the problem, tested solutions, and collaborated with developers to implement fixes.

2. How do you stay informed about the latest developments and updates in the mac OS ecosystem, and how do you apply this knowledge to your role?

Answer:I regularly follow Apple's developer documentation, participate in relevant forums, and attend conferences to stay updated. I apply this knowledge by implementing best practices and ensuring compatibility with the latest mac OS versions.

Collaboration and Teamwork:

1. Describe your experience collaborating with cross-functional teams, such as designers and QA, in the development of mac OS features or applications.

Answer:I have a proven track record of collaborating with diverse teams. For example, I worked closely with designers to ensure that mac OS applications adhered to design guidelines, resulting in a cohesive user experience.

2. How do you approach communication within a development team, especially when dealing with complex technical concepts?

Answer: Communication is crucial. I break down complex technical concepts into understandable terms, encourage open dialogue, and provide documentation to ensure everyone on the team has a clear understanding of the project.

Project Management:

1. Discuss your experience with project management tools and methodologies, and how you ensure the successful delivery of mac OS projects on time and within scope.

Answer:I am well-versed in project management tools like Jira and methodologies such as Agile. I emphasize regular communication, set clear expectations, and prioritize tasks to ensure project milestones are met.

2. How do you approach the planning and execution of software updates and releases for mac OS applications, considering potential user impact and system compatibility?

Answer:I follow a structured release process, including thorough testing on different mac OS versions, monitoring user feedback, and addressing issues promptly. This approach minimizes disruptions and ensures a smooth user experience.

Adaptability and Learning:

1. How do you stay adaptable in the face of rapidly evolving technologies, and how do you approach learning new tools or programming languages?

Answer:I have a proactive approach to learning. I allocate time for continuous education, stay informed about industry trends, and actively seek opportunities to apply new technologies in my work.

2. Share an example of a time when you had to quickly learn and apply a new technology or framework to meet project requirements.

Answer: In a previous project, we needed to implement a new framework to improve application performance. I immersed myself in learning the framework, conducted training sessions for the team, and successfully integrated it into our workflow.

Leadership and Mentorship:

1. Have you had experience leading or mentoring junior developers? If so, how do you approach guiding and supporting less experienced team members?

Answer: Yes, I have experience in mentoring. I approach mentorship by providing guidance, encouraging questions, and creating an environment where team members feel comfortable seeking help. I also emphasize continuous learning and skill development.

2. How do you foster a collaborative and positive team culture, and how does this contribute to the success of mac OS development projects?

Answer:A positive team culture is essential for productivity and creativity. I promote open communication, celebrate achievements, and encourage a collaborative atmosphere where team members feel empowered to share ideas and solutions.

Ethics and Compliance:

1. How do you ensure that your work complies with ethical standards, especially considering user privacy and data security?

Answer:I adhere to ethical coding practices, prioritize user privacy, and comply with relevant regulations. I stay informed about industry standards and work closely with legal and compliance teams to ensure our applications meet ethical guidelines.

2. Discuss the importance of maintaining a secure and compliant development environment, especially in the context of mac OS application development.

Answer: Security and compliance are paramount. I ensure that development environments adhere to security best practices, conduct regular code reviews, and implement measures to safeguard user data and privacy.

Remote Work and Collaboration:

1. How do you ensure effective collaboration and communication when working remotely on mac OS development projects?

Answer: Remote collaboration requires robust communication tools and regular check-ins. I leverage video conferencing, collaboration platforms, and maintain transparent documentation to keep the team aligned and informed.

2. Discuss the challenges and opportunities you've encountered in adapting mac OS development processes to accommodate remote work trends.

Answer: Remote work has highlighted the importance of asynchronous communication and flexible project management. While it presents challenges, it also offers opportunities for a more diverse and globally distributed talent pool.

Innovation and Creativity:

1. Share an example of how you've contributed to the innovation of mac OS applications or features, either through design improvements or the implementation of new technologies.

Answer: In a previous role, I played a key role in implementing a new feature that significantly improved the efficiency of file handling in mac OS. This involved creative problem-solving and collaboration with the design team.

2. How do you approach balancing innovation with maintaining a stable and reliable user experience in mac OS applications?

Answer: Balancing innovation and stability is crucial. I advocate for a phased approach to innovation, ensuring that new features undergo rigorous testing and user feedback before becoming integral parts of the user experience.

3. As a seasoned mac OS developer, how do you see your role evolving in the future, and what steps are you taking to stay ahead in the ever-changing landscape of software development?

Answer:I see my role evolving with a continued focus on embracing new technologies, staying informed about industry trends, and contributing to the development of innovative solutions. I prioritize continuous learning and professional development to stay at the forefront of mac OS development.

Mac OS Architecture

mac OS Architecture Overview:

1. Can you provide an overview of the architecture of mac OS, highlighting key components and their interactions?

Answer:mac OS follows a layered architecture. At its core is the Darwin kernel, on top of which layers like Core Services, Media, and Cocoa provide frameworks. The Window Server manages the graphical user interface, while user applications interact with these layers.

2. Explain the role of the Mach microkernel in the mac OS architecture.

Answer: The Mach microkernel handles core tasks like process management and inter-process communication. It acts as the foundation for the overall mac OS kernel, providing essential services for the operating system.

3. Discuss the significance of the UNIX underpinnings in mac OS and how it influences the architecture of the operating system.

Answer:mac OS inherits key UNIX features, including a hierarchical file system, command-line interface, and multi-user capabilities. This UNIX foundation contributes to the stability and security of the operating system.

4. How does the mac OS architecture support the integration of different hardware components, considering the diversity of Mac devices?

Answer:mac OS utilizes device drivers to interface with diverse hardware components. The I/O Kit framework facilitates communication between drivers and the operating system, ensuring compatibility with various Mac hardware configurations.

Kernel and System Components:

1. Explain the role of the XNU kernel in mac OS and how it manages tasks like memory management and process scheduling.

Answer:XNU is a hybrid kernel that combines elements of the Mach microkernel with components from FreeBSD and C++. It manages tasks such as memory allocation, process scheduling, and device management.

2. How does mac OS handle virtual memory management, and what mechanisms are in place to optimize memory usage?

Answer:mac OS uses a demand-paging system for virtual memory management. Techniques like memory compression, swapping, and dynamic pager management are employed to optimize memory usage and enhance system performance.

3. Discuss the role of the I/O Kit framework in mac OS and how it facilitates communication between the operating system and device drivers.

Answer: The I/O Kit framework is crucial for developing device drivers. It provides a set of C++ classes and APIs for interacting with hardware components, ensuring a standardized approach to device communication.

4. How does mac OS handle system calls, and what is the significance of the System Call Interface (SCI) in the operating system's architecture?

Answer: System calls in mac OS are handled through the SCI, which provides a bridge between user-space applications and the kernel. It defines the interface for processes to request services from the kernel, ensuring a secure and controlled interaction.

File System and Storage:

1.Explain the architecture of the HFS+ file system and its evolution to the APFS (Apple File System) in recent mac OS versions.

Answer:HFS+ was the traditional file system, and APFS was introduced to address limitations and provide modern features such as enhanced performance, encryption, and snapshots.

2. How does mac OS handle storage management, and what role do technologies like Fusion Drive and Core Storage play in optimizing storage performance?

Answer: Fusion Drive combines SSD and HDD for improved performance, while Core Storage enables features like FileVault encryption and logical volume management, contributing to optimized storage performance.

3. Discuss the impact of technologies like Time Machine on the architecture of mac OS and how they facilitate data backup and recovery.

Answer: Time Machine utilizes a backup-on-write mechanism, storing incremental changes to provide a complete backup history. This architecture ensures efficient data backup and simplified recovery for users.

4. Explain how mac OS supports external storage devices and how the Plug and Play architecture enhances user experience.

Answer:mac OS supports external storage through the Plug and Play architecture, allowing users to connect devices like external hard drives or USB sticks. The operating system recognizes and configures these devices without requiring manual intervention.

Graphics and Display:

1. Discuss the role of the Core Graphics framework in mac OS and how it facilitates rendering and manipulation of graphical content.

Answer: Core Graphics provides a high-level API for rendering 2D graphics. It includes features for drawing paths, handling transformations, and working with color spaces, contributing to the overall graphics rendering in mac OS.

2. How does mac OS manage graphical user interfaces, and what role does the WindowServer play in rendering and displaying application windows?

Answer: The WindowServer is responsible for managing the graphical user interface. It handles tasks such as window composition, rendering, and display management, ensuring a responsive and visually appealing user experience.

3. Discuss the significance of Metal in mac OS and how it optimizes graphics performance, especially in the context of gaming and multimedia applications.

Answer: Metal is a low-level graphics API that provides direct access to the GPU. It optimizes graphics performance by reducing overhead, making it ideal for resource-intensive tasks like gaming and multimedia applications.

4. How does mac OS handle multiple displays, and what role does the Graphics Switching technology play in optimizing power consumption on Mac laptops?

Answer:mac OS supports multiple displays through features like Mission Control and Spaces. Graphics Switching technology allows laptops with dual GPUs to switch between integrated and discrete graphics based on the task, optimizing power consumption.

Application Frameworks:

1. Explain the role of the Cocoa framework in mac OS application development and how it facilitates the creation of user interfaces.

Answer: Cocoa is a key framework for mac OS application development, providing a set of APIs for creating user interfaces, handling events, and managing application lifecycle. It is based on the Objective-C language.

2. Discuss the evolution of application frameworks in mac OS, especially the introduction of SwiftUI and its impact on modern application development.

Answer: SwiftUI is a declarative framework introduced to simplify UI development. It allows developers to create dynamic interfaces with less code. Its introduction marks a shift toward more modern and efficient application development in mac OS.

3. How does mac OS support cross-platform development, and what role does Catalyst play in enabling the creation of apps that run on both mac OS and iOS?

Answer: Catalyst enables developers to use a common codebase to create apps that run on both mac OS and iOS. It streamlines development, providing a unified approach to designing and deploying applications across Apple platforms.

Security and Privacy:

1. Discuss the security architecture of mac OS, including features like Gatekeeper, FileVault, and the Secure Enclave.

Answer: Gatekeeper ensures only trusted software runs on a Mac, FileVault provides full-disk encryption, and the Secure Enclave enhances security for features like Touch ID and Apple Pay, collectively creating a robust security architecture.

2. How does mac OS address privacy concerns, and what role does the App Sandbox play in limiting an application's access to user data?

Answer: App Sandbox restricts an application's access to system resources and user data, enhancing privacy and security. mac OS also incorporates privacy features like app permissions and user consent prompts.

Networking and Connectivity:

1. Explain how mac OS handles network protocols and how technologies like Bonjour facilitate seamless device discovery and communication on local networks.

Answer:mac OS supports various network protocols, and Bonjour simplifies device discovery and communication on local networks. It enables automatic service discovery and network configuration.

2. Discuss the role of Core Networking in mac OS and how it provides developers with APIs for building network-related features in their applications.

Answer: Core Networking is a framework that provides a set of APIs for building network-related features. It simplifies tasks such as establishing connections, handling protocols, and managing network resources.

Performance Optimization:

1. How does mac OS optimize system performance, and what role do technologies like Grand Central Dispatch play in managing concurrency and parallelism?

Answer: Grand Central Dispatch optimizes system performance by efficiently managing tasks across multiple cores. It enables developers to implement concurrency and parallelism, enhancing overall system responsiveness.

2. Discuss the significance of technologies like Metal for GPU acceleration and how they contribute to performance optimization in graphics-intensive applications.

Answer: Metal provides direct access to the GPU, reducing overhead and optimizing graphics performance. It is particularly beneficial for graphics-intensive applications, such as video editing and 3D rendering.

Virtualization and Emulation:

1. How does mac OS support virtualization, and what role does Hypervisor.framework play in enabling the virtualization of multiple operating systems on a Mac?

Answer: Hypervisor.framework allows developers to create and manage virtual machines on mac OS. It enables the virtualization of multiple operating systems, facilitating tasks such as software testing and development.

2. Discuss the integration of technologies like Rosetta 2 in mac OS, and how it facilitates the emulation of applications designed for different processor architectures.

Answer: Rosetta 2 is an emulation technology that allows Macs with Apple Silicon to run applications designed for Intel processors. It seamlessly translates code, enabling compatibility with legacy software.

Software Development and Debugging:

1. How does mac OS support software development, and what role do tools like Xcode play in the development lifecycle?

Answer: Xcode is the primary integrated development environment (IDE) for mac OS. It provides tools for coding, debugging, and profiling applications, as well as managing project resources and dependencies.

2. Explain the debugging tools available in Xcode and how they assist developers in identifying and resolving issues in their mac OS applications.

Answer: Xcode offers a range of debugging tools, including LLDB for code-level debugging, Instruments for performance analysis, and the visual debugger for tracking UI issues. These tools aid in identifying and resolving application issues.

System Updates and Versioning:

1. How does mac OS handle system updates, and what mechanisms are in place to ensure a smooth transition for users when upgrading to a new version of the operating system?

Answer:mac OS uses the Software Update mechanism to deliver system updates. It ensures a smooth transition by providing compatibility checks, offering clear user prompts, and allowing users to roll back updates if issues arise.

2. Discuss the versioning strategy of mac OS, including how version numbers are assigned and the significance of incremental updates versus major releases.

Answer:mac OS versioning typically follows a major.minor.patch format. Major releases introduce significant changes, while incremental updates focus on bug fixes, security patches, and minor enhancements.

System Integration and Continuity:

1. How does mac OS facilitate the continuity of user experiences across different Apple devices, and what role do features like Handoff and Universal Clipboard play in this integration?

Answer: Features like Handoff and Universal Clipboard enable continuity by allowing users to seamlessly transition between Macs, iPhones, and iPads. They ensure a cohesive and uninterrupted user experience across Apple devices.

2. Discuss the integration of Siri into mac OS and how it enhances user productivity through voice commands and system-wide interactions.

Answer: Siri is integrated into mac OS to provide voice-driven commands and system-wide interactions. It enhances user productivity by allowing hands-free control and access to information.

Machine Learning and AI:

1. Explain how mac OS integrates machine learning capabilities, and what role does the Core ML framework play in enabling developers to incorporate machine learning models into their applications?

Answer: Core ML allows developers to integrate machine learning models into mac OS applications. It provides a unified interface for using pre-trained models, enhancing the integration of machine learning capabilities into various applications.

2. Discuss the significance of Metal Performance Shaders (MPS) in mac OS and how they accelerate the development of machine learning and image processing applications.

Answer: Metal Performance Shaders provide a set of highly optimized libraries for machine learning and image processing tasks. They leverage the power of the GPU to accelerate performance, making it easier for developers to implement advanced features.

Accessibility and Inclusivity:

1. How does mac OS address accessibility concerns, and what role do features like VoiceOver and Accessibility APIs play in making the operating system inclusive for users with diverse needs?

Answer: Features like VoiceOver provide auditory feedback, while Accessibility APIs enable developers to create applications accessible to users with diverse needs. These features are integral to ensuring inclusivity in mac OS.

2. Discuss the role of Dynamic Type in mac OS and how it contributes to the accessibility and readability of text across different applications.

Answer: Dynamic Type allows users to adjust the system-wide text size, ensuring readability for individuals with visual impairments. It contributes to the overall accessibility of mac OS applications.

Future Developments:

1. What do you foresee as the future trends in the architecture of mac OS, considering advancements in hardware technology and changing user expectations?

Answer:I anticipate continued integration with Apple Silicon, further advancements in machine learning integration, and a focus on enhancing cross-platform development to create a seamless user experience across all Apple devices.

2. How might the ongoing transition to Apple Silicon influence the architecture of mac OS in the coming years, and what challenges and opportunities do you anticipate?

Answer: The transition to Apple Silicon will likely result in a more unified architecture across Apple devices, with opportunities for improved performance and energy efficiency. Challenges may include ensuring compatibility with existing software and optimizing workflows for the new architecture.

Troubleshooting and Optimization:

1. Share experiences where you've been involved in troubleshooting complex architectural issues on mac OS, and how you approached problem-solving and optimization.

Answer: In a previous role, I encountered performance issues related to memory management. I conducted thorough profiling, identified bottlenecks, and implemented optimizations in the code. Collaboration with the development and QA teams ensured a successful resolution.

ONLINE RESOURCES

Practice Paper Link: https://forms.gle/abC58PvXkC4D4GQW7

QR Code:

Video Link: https://www.youtube.com/playlist?list=PLzlh_31VWEFoRsAoogmEKdH0PSKSlA9c9

QR Code:

Chapter 2: mac OS Fundamentals

File System Structure

Basic Concepts:

1. What is the role of a file system in macOS?

Answer: The file system in macOS manages how data is stored, organized, and retrieved on storage devices.

2. Can you explain the difference between HFS+ and APFS?

Answer:HFS+ is the older file system used in macOS, while APFS (Apple File System) is the newer, optimized file system with features like snapshots, encryption, and improved performance.

3. How does macOS handle file permissions, and what are the common permission levels?

Answer:macOS uses a combination of owner, group, and others' permissions. Common permission levels include read, write, and execute.

File System Structure:

1.Describe the directory structure of macOS.

Answer:macOS follows a hierarchical file system structure with the root directory ("/") at the top, containing system and user directories.

2. What is the purpose of the /Applications and /System folders in macOS?

Answer:/Applications contains user-installed applications, while /System contains core system files and applications.

3. Explain the purpose of the /Users directory.

Answer:/Users stores user-specific data, including home directories for each user account.

4. How does macOS manage symbolic links, and what is their purpose?

Answer: Symbolic links are pointers to other files or directories. They provide a way to reference files or directories in different locations.

Storage and Volumes:

1. What is the difference between a hard link and a soft link (symlink) in macOS?

Answer: Hard links point directly to the inode of a file, while symlinks are separate files that point to the target file by its path.

2. How does macOS manage disk volumes, and what is the role of Disk Utility?

Answer: Disk Utility is used to manage disk volumes. macOS supports creating, formatting, and managing volumes on different storage devices.

3. Explain the concept of Fusion Drive in macOS.

Answer: Fusion Drive is a hybrid storage solution that combines SSD and HDD to optimize performance and storage capacity.

File Attributes and Metadata:

1. What is file metadata, and how is it stored in macOS?

Answer: File metadata includes information about a file (e.g., creation date, size). macOS stores metadata in extended attributes.

2. How does macOS handle file timestamps, and what are the different timestamps associated with a file?

Answer:macOS maintains three timestamps for each file: creation time, modification time, and access time.

3. Can you explain how macOS uses resource forks and data forks in file storage?

Answer: Resource forks and data forks were used in older macOS file systems for storing additional file information. In modern macOS (APFS), this information is handled differently.

Permissions and Security:

1. How does macOS enforce file permissions?

Answer:macOS enforces file permissions through the user, group, and other permission settings. Only users with appropriate permissions can access or modify files.

2. What is the purpose of the root user in macOS, and how can it be enabled?

Answer: The root user has superuser privileges. It can be enabled in the Directory Utility or by using the sudo command in the Terminal.

3. Explain the role of FileVault in macOS.

Answer: FileVault is macOS's disk encryption program. It encrypts the entire startup disk to enhance data security.

Command-Line Tools:

1. How can you list files and directories in the Terminal?

Answer: The ls command is used to list files and directories in the Terminal.

2. What is the purpose of the cd command in the Terminal?

Answer: The cd command is used to change the current working directory in the Terminal.

3. How do you create a symbolic link in the Terminal?

Answer: The ln -s command is used to create symbolic links in the Terminal.

Performance and Optimization:

1. How can you check disk usage in macOS?

Answer: The df and du commands in the Terminal can be used to check disk usage.

2. Explain the role of TRIM in SSD optimization.

Answer:TRIM is a command that helps optimize the performance of SSDs by informing the drive which blocks are no longer in use.

3. How can you optimize the performance of a Mac with a large number of files?

Answer: Strategies include using SSDs, organizing files into folders, and regularly performing maintenance tasks.

Backups and Recovery:

1. What is Time Machine, and how does it work?

Answer: Time Machine is macOS's built-in backup solution. It creates incremental backups, allowing users to restore files or the entire system to previous states.

2. Explain the process of restoring a file from a Time Machine backup.

Answer: Users can enter Time Machine, navigate to the desired date, and select the file for restoration.

3. How does macOS handle file versioning?

Answer:macOS supports file versioning, which allows users to access previous versions of a file through the "Versions" feature.

Advanced Topics:

1. What is the role of Journaling in macOS file systems?

Answer: Journaling helps maintain file system integrity by recording changes before they are applied, reducing the risk of data corruption.

2. Explain the concept of snapshots in APFS.

Answer: Snapshots are read-only copies of a file system at a specific point in time. They provide a way to revert to a previous state.

3. How can you repair a disk using the Disk Utility or Terminal?

Answer: Disk Utility provides a graphical interface, while the fsck command in the Terminal can be used for disk repair.

Troubleshooting:

1. What steps would you take to troubleshoot file system issues on a Mac?

Answer: Steps may include checking disk permissions, running Disk Utility, and using Terminal commands like fsck.

2. How can you identify and resolve file permission conflicts in macOS?

Answer: The chmod command can be used to adjust file permissions. Additionally, checking and adjusting user and group ownership may resolve conflicts.

3. Explain how to diagnose and address disk space issues on a Mac.

Answer: Use commands like df and du in the Terminal to identify space-consuming directories. Removing unnecessary files and applications can free up space.

Networking and File Sharing:

1. How does macOS handle network file sharing, and what protocols are involved?

Answer:macOS supports file sharing over the SMB (Server Message Block) and AFP (Apple Filing Protocol) protocols.

2. What is the purpose of the macOS "Shared" folder, and how can files be shared?

Answer: The "Shared" folder is a central location for sharing files. Users can enable file sharing in System Preferences and configure access permissions.

Integration with Other Technologies:

1. How does macOS integrate with iCloud for file storage?

Answer:macOS users can store documents and files in iCloud Drive, providing seamless access across multiple devices.

2. Explain how Time Machine integrates with external storage devices.

Answer: Time Machine can use external drives for backups. Users select an external drive as the backup destination in Time Machine settings.

Scripting and Automation:

1. How can you automate file-related tasks in macOS using scripts?

Answer:macOS supports scripting languages like Bash and AppleScript. Users can create scripts to automate repetitive file tasks.

2. Provide an example of a Terminal command to find and delete files older than a certain date.

Answer: The find and rm commands can be combined, e.g., find . -type f -mtime +30 -exec rm {} \; to delete files older than 30 days.

Future Trends and Updates:

1. What changes or improvements have been introduced in recent macOS updates related to file systems?

Answer:macOS updates may introduce improvements to file system performance, security, and compatibility. Stay informed about the latest release notes.

2. How do you stay updated on advancements in macOS file systems and technologies?

Answer: Regularly following Apple's documentation, release notes, and participating in developer communities and forums helps stay informed.

3. In your opinion, what could be potential future developments in macOS file systems?

Answer: Speculative answers could include advancements in encryption, integration with emerging technologies, or improvements in handling large-scale data.

User Interface Elements

Basic Concepts:

1. What are the key principles of macOS user interface design?

Answer:macOS UI design emphasizes clarity, consistency, and simplicity. It follows the Human Interface Guidelines (HIG) to provide a seamless and intuitive user experience.

2. Explain the role of the Dock in macOS.

Answer: The Dock is a central UI element that provides quick access to frequently used applications and features. It's located at the bottom of the screen by default.

3. How does the macOS menu bar contribute to the overall user experience?

Answer: The menu bar at the top of the screen contains application-specific menus, providing a standardized and easily accessible way for users to navigate and control applications.

Window Management:

1. Describe the purpose of the title bar in macOS windows.

Answer: The title bar displays the name of the active document or application and contains the close, minimize, and maximize buttons for window management.

2. How does macOS handle window resizing and what is the role of the green button in the title bar?

Answer: The green button maximizes the window to its optimal size, or, in some applications, it may trigger a specific resizing behavior defined by the app.

3. Explain the concept of Mission Control in macOS.

Answer: Mission Control provides a bird's-eye view of open applications, windows, and spaces, facilitating efficient navigation and organization.

4. What are Spaces in macOS, and how can they enhance multitasking?

Answer: Spaces allow users to organize and separate open applications into different virtual desktops, improving multitasking and decluttering the workspace.

Application Interface Design:

1. How does macOS encourage the use of standard UI elements across applications?

Answer:macOS follows the Human Interface Guidelines (HIG), providing a set of design principles and standard UI elements to ensure consistency across applications.

2. Explain the purpose of the Toolbar in macOS applications.

Answer: The Toolbar contains commonly used actions and tools specific to the application, offering quick access to frequently used functions.

3. How does macOS support document-centric applications, and what is the role of the Document Browser?

Answer: Document-centric applications in macOS allow users to work with multiple documents simultaneously. The Document Browser provides an organized view of open documents.

Controls and Views:

1. Describe the various UI controls available in macOS applications.

Answer: Common UI controls include buttons, sliders, text fields, checkboxes, radio buttons, and more, which can be customized based on the application's needs.

2. How does macOS handle text input and editing, and what are the standard text editing features?

Answer:macOS supports rich text editing with features such as copy-paste, undo-redo, and spell checking. NSTextView is a key class for text handling.

3. Explain the purpose of the NSImageView class in macOS.

Answer:NSImageView is a class used for displaying images in macOS applications. It supports various image formats and provides features like scaling and animation.

Accessibility and Inclusivity:

1. How does macOS address accessibility in user interface design?

Answer:macOS includes accessibility features like VoiceOver, Magnifier, and Zoom to ensure that applications are usable by individuals with varying abilities.

2. What considerations should be taken into account for designing an inclusive user interface?

Answer: Inclusive UI design involves providing alternative text for images, ensuring proper color contrast, and supporting keyboard navigation for users with disabilities.

3. Explain the role of the Accessibility Inspector in macOS development.

Answer: The Accessibility Inspector is a tool that helps developers ensure their applications are accessible by providing information about the accessibility properties of UI elements.

Animation and Transitions:

1. How can animation enhance the user experience in macOS applications?

Answer: Well-designed animations can provide feedback, guide users' attention, and create a more engaging and intuitive interface.

2. What are Core Animation layers, and how do they contribute to UI animation in macOS?

Answer: Core Animation layers are lightweight objects used to animate views and graphics efficiently. They enable smooth animations and transitions.

3. Explain the role of the CA Animation class in macOS.

Answer:CA Animation is a class in Core Animation that defines the properties and timing of an animation. It is used to create a variety of animations in macOS applications.

User Interaction and Feedback:

1. How does macOS handle user input from mouse and trackpad gestures?

Answer:macOS recognizes various gestures, such as scrolling, pinching, and swiping, providing users with intuitive ways to interact with applications.

3. Describe the purpose of the NSResponder class in macOS application development.

Answer:NSResponder is the base class for objects that respond to user events. It plays a crucial role in handling user input and responding to actions.

4. What are the best practices for providing feedback to users in macOS applications?

Answer: Feedback should be immediate and informative. Visual cues, such as animations or status messages, can enhance the user experience.

Integration with System Features:

1. How can macOS applications integrate with system-wide services like Siri or Spotlight?

Answer: Developers can leverage AppKit frameworks to integrate with system services, making their applications more accessible and versatile.

2. Explain the role of the Touch Bar in MacBook Pro models and how it can be utilized in application development.

Answer: The Touch Bar provides context-sensitive controls and shortcuts, and developers can customize it to enhance their applications with relevant features.

Theming and Customization:

1. How can developers provide users with options for customizing the appearance of an application in macOS?

Answer: Developers can use NSAppearance and NSAppearanceCustomization protocols to allow users to choose between light and dark modes, among other customization options.

2. Describe the role of Interface Builder in designing user interfaces for macOS applications.

Answer: Interface Builder is a visual design tool that allows developers to design, connect, and configure UI elements for macOS applications.

3. What considerations should be taken into account when designing a user interface that supports both macOS and iOS platforms?

Answer: Designing for cross-platform compatibility involves considering differences in screen size, input methods, and platform-specific design guidelines.

Advanced Topics:

1. How can a developer implement drag-and-drop functionality in a macOS application?

Answer: Developers can implement drag-and-drop by conforming to the NSDraggingDestination and NSDraggingSource protocols, providing a seamless user experience for moving or copying data.

2. Explain the role of SwiftUI in macOS UI development.

Answer: SwiftUI is a declarative UI framework that simplifies the development of UI elements and interactions, making it easier for developers to create dynamic and responsive interfaces.

3. What is the role of Catalyst in macOS application development, and how does it impact the user interface?

Answer: Catalyst allows developers to bring iPad apps to the Mac, providing a consistent user interface and user experience across both platforms.

Usability Testing and User Feedback:

1. How do you approach usability testing for a macOS application, and what methods do you find effective?

Answer: Usability testing involves observing users interact with the application and collecting feedback to identify areas for improvement. Methods may include interviews, surveys, and task analysis.

2. Describe a situation where user feedback significantly influenced the design of a macOS application you worked on.

Answer: Provide a specific example of how user feedback led to positive changes in the application's design, functionality, or usability.

3. How do you balance user feedback with design principles and technical constraints when making UI decisions?

Answer: Balancing user feedback with design principles and technical constraints requires prioritization. Decisions should align with the overall goals of the application and the user experience.

Integration with App Store Guidelines:

1. How do you ensure that your macOS application complies with Apple's App Store guidelines regarding user interface design?

Answer: Regularly reviewing and adhering to the Human Interface Guidelines (HIG) and App Store guidelines helps ensure compliance. Thorough testing and adherence to best practices are also essential.

2. What are the key considerations when designing the first-run experience for a macOS application?

Answer: The first-run experience should be intuitive and guide users through essential setup steps. It's an opportunity to showcase the application's features and set a positive tone.

Security and Privacy:

1. How can developers ensure that user interface elements align with macOS security and privacy standards?

Answer:UI elements should clearly communicate security features, such as SSL/TLS indicators, and respect user privacy by requesting necessary permissions and providing transparent data handling practices.

2. Explain the role of the Keychain in macOS applications and how it contributes to a secure user experience.

Answer: The Keychain securely stores sensitive information such as passwords and cryptographic keys, enhancing the security of macOS applications.

Collaboration and Teamwork:

1. Describe a situation where you collaborated with designers or other developers to achieve a cohesive user interface in a macOS application.

Answer: Collaboration may involve discussing design decisions, providing feedback, and iterating on UI elements to ensure consistency and alignment with the application's goals.

2. How do you approach providing UI documentation for other team members or future maintainers of your code?

Answer: Providing clear and comprehensive documentation, including design rationale, UI component details, and interactions, helps facilitate collaboration and maintainability.

Future Trends and Updates:

1. In your opinion, what could be potential future developments in macOS user interface elements?

Answer: Speculative answers could include advancements in augmented reality (AR) interfaces, integration with new input methods, or further evolution of SwiftUI for even more streamlined UI development.

System Preferences

Basic Concepts:

1. What is the purpose of System Preferences in macOS?

Answer: System Preferences is the centralized hub for configuring and customizing various settings on a Mac, including system, network, security, and user preferences.

2. Explain the difference between System Preferences and individual application preferences.

Answer: System Preferences manage global settings for the entire system, while individual application preferences are specific to each application.

3. How can you access System Preferences on a Mac?

Answer: System Preferences can be accessed through the Apple menu or by clicking the System Preferences icon in the Dock.

General System Settings:

1. What options are available in the "General" pane of System Preferences?

Answer: The "General" pane includes settings for appearance, accent color, highlight color, and sidebar icon size.

2. Explain the purpose of the "Desktop & Screen Saver" preferences.

Answer: This section allows users to customize their desktop background and configure screen savers.

3. How can you customize the appearance of the Dock using System Preferences?

Answer: Users can modify Dock preferences to change its size, position, and enable features like magnification.

4. What options are available in the "Energy Saver" preferences, and how do they impact system performance?

Answer:"Energy Saver" settings allow users to manage power-related features, such as sleep mode and display sleep, to optimize energy usage.

User Accounts and Security:

1. Describe the user account management options in the "Users & Groups" preferences.

Answer:"Users & Groups" allows users to manage user accounts, set login items, and configure user-specific preferences.

2. What security features can be configured in the "Security & Privacy" preferences?

Answer: This pane includes settings for firewall, FileVault disk encryption, and privacy preferences for applications.

3. How does the "Parental Controls" feature in System Preferences work?

Answer: "Parental Controls" allows users to restrict access to certain applications and content for specific user accounts, making it suitable for parental guidance.

Hardware and Peripherals:

1. What options are available in the "Printers & Scanners" preferences, and how can users add new printers?

Answer: Users can add and manage printers, scanners, and fax machines in this pane, configuring print settings and managing print queues.

2. How does the "Bluetooth" preferences pane contribute to device connectivity?

Answer: "Bluetooth" preferences allow users to pair and manage Bluetooth devices, such as keyboards, mice, and headphones.

3. Explain the purpose of the "Sound" preferences and how users can customize audio settings.

Answer: "Sound" preferences control audio input and output settings, allowing users to configure speakers, microphones, and sound effects.

4. What options are available in the "Keyboard" preferences, and how can users customize keyboard shortcuts?

Answer: Users can modify keyboard settings, such as key repeat rate, and customize shortcuts in the "Keyboard" preferences.

Network and Internet:

1. Describe the functions of the "Network" preferences pane.

Answer: "Network" preferences manage network connections, including Wi-Fi, Ethernet, and VPN settings.

2. How can users configure email accounts and manage mail settings in the "Internet Accounts" preferences?

Answer: "Internet Accounts" allows users to add and manage email accounts, syncing contacts, calendars, and more.

3. Explain the purpose of the "Sharing" preferences and the options available for sharing resources.

Answer: "Sharing" preferences control file sharing, screen sharing, and other sharing services on the Mac.

4. How does the "Network Utility" application complement the "Network" preferences?

Answer: "Network Utility" provides additional tools for troubleshooting network-related issues, complementing the configuration options in "Network" preferences.

System Updates and Time Machine:

1. How can users configure automatic updates for macOS in the "Software Update" preferences?

Answer: Users can set preferences for automatic updates, ensuring the system and apps are kept up-to-date.

2. Explain the purpose of the "Time Machine" preferences, and how does it contribute to data backup?

Answer:"Time Machine" preferences allow users to set up and manage automatic backups, ensuring data recovery in case of system failure.

Accessibility:

1. Describe the accessibility features available in the "Accessibility" preferences.

Answer:"Accessibility" preferences include options for vision, hearing, and motor skills, providing a more inclusive experience for users with different abilities.

2. How can users configure VoiceOver settings in System Preferences?

Answer: Users can enable and customize VoiceOver, a screen-reading feature, in the "Accessibility" preferences.

Internationalization and Language Preferences:

1. What options are available in the "Language & Region" preferences?

Answer: Users can configure language preferences, region settings, and date/time formats in this pane.

2. Explain the purpose of the "Keyboard" preferences under "Language & Region."

Answer:"Keyboard" preferences allow users to configure keyboard input methods and language preferences.

Security and Privacy:

1. How does the "Privacy" preferences contribute to user security?

Answer:"Privacy" preferences allow users to manage application access to sensitive data, such as location services, contacts, and files.

2. What is Gatekeeper, and how can users configure its settings in the "Security & Privacy" preferences?

Answer: Gatekeeper is a security feature that controls app installations. Users can configure it in "Security & Privacy" preferences to allow apps from the App Store or identified developers.

Siri and Dictation:

1. How can users enable and configure Siri in the "Siri" preferences?

Answer: Users can enable Siri and customize its settings, including language, voice, and voice feedback, in the "Siri" preferences.

2. Describe the role of the "Dictation" preferences in macOS.

Answer:"Dictation" preferences allow users to enable and configure voice dictation, converting spoken words into text.

Advanced Topics:

1. What is the role of the Terminal in configuring system preferences beyond the GUI?

Answer: The Terminal allows advanced users to configure system preferences using command-line tools, providing more granular control.

2. How can users customize the system appearance using Terminal commands?

Answer: Terminal commands, such as defaults write and killall, can be used to modify system appearance settings not available in the System Preferences GUI.

Troubleshooting:

1. What steps would you take to troubleshoot issues with network connectivity in the "Network" preferences?

Answer: Troubleshooting steps may include checking network cables, resetting network configurations, and using the "Network Utility" for diagnostics.

2. How can users troubleshoot Time Machine backup issues using System Preferences and other tools?

Answer: Troubleshooting Time Machine issues may involve checking disk space, verifying backup disk connections, and using the "Time Machine" preferences for diagnostics.

Integration with Other Technologies:

1. How does Handoff work, and how can users enable it in the "General" preferences?

Answer: Handoff allows users to seamlessly transition tasks between Apple devices. It can be enabled in the "General" preferences.

2. Explain the integration of iCloud in various System Preferences panes.

Answer:iCloud integration is present in settings such as "Apple ID," "iCloud," and "Internet Accounts," providing synchronization of data across Apple devices.

Customization and Automation:

1. How can users create custom keyboard shortcuts for specific actions in macOS applications?

Answer: Users can define custom keyboard shortcuts in the "Keyboard" preferences, under the "Shortcuts" tab.

2. What is Automator, and how can it be used to automate tasks related to System Preferences?

Answer: Automator is a tool for creating automated workflows. Users can create workflows that include actions related to System Preferences tasks.

Collaboration and Teamwork:

1. How would you guide a less experienced team member in navigating and configuring System Preferences for a specific task?

Answer: Provide guidance on where to find relevant settings in System Preferences, explain the purpose of each preference pane, and offer tips for efficient configuration.

2. Describe a situation where you collaborated with other team members to troubleshoot a System Preferences-related issue.

Answer: Share a specific example of identifying and resolving a System Preferences issue collaboratively, demonstrating effective teamwork.

Future Trends and Updates:

1. In your opinion, what could be potential future developments in macOS System Preferences?

Answer: Speculative answers could include improvements in user interface design, new features for system management, or integration with emerging technologies.

2. How do you stay updated on advancements and changes in macOS System Preferences and settings?

Answer: Staying informed through Apple's official documentation, release notes, and participating in developer communities and forums helps keep up with the latest updates.

ONLINE RESOURCES

Practice Paper Link: https://forms.gle/pVwPQXURUVpHjbvP7

QR Code:

Video Link: https://www.youtube.com/playlist?list=PLzlh_31VWEFqk6XUc8iCNB0vW2J4Y3CSA

QR Code:

Chapter 3: mac OS File System

Understanding the File System Hierarchy

Basics of macOS File System:

1. What is the file system hierarchy in macOS?

Answer: The file system hierarchy in macOS follows a tree structure with the root directory ("/") at the top, branching into various directories like /Applications, /Users, and /System.

2. Explain the purpose of the /Applications directory.

Answer:/Applications is where macOS stores applications installed for all users on the system.

3. How does macOS handle user-specific data?

Answer: User-specific data is stored in the /Users directory, with each user having their own home directory.

Directory Structure:

1. What is the purpose of the /Library directory in macOS?

Answer:/Library contains system-wide libraries and resources shared by all users.

2. Differentiate between /System and /Library.

Answer:/System contains core system files, while /Library contains shared resources and libraries.

3. Explain the significance of the /private directory.

Answer:/private is used for system-critical files and should not be modified by users.

Permissions and Security:

1. How are file permissions managed in macOS?

Answer:macOS uses a combination of user, group, and other permissions (rwx) to control access to files and directories.

2. What is the significance of the sudo command in macOS?

Answer:sudo allows users to execute commands with administrative privileges.

3. How can you check and modify file permissions in macOS?

Answer: Use the ls -l command to view permissions and the chmod command to modify them.

File Types and Extensions:

1. Differentiate between a regular file and a symbolic link.

Answer:A regular file contains data, while a symbolic link is a reference to another file or directory.

2. What is the purpose of file extensions in macOS?

Answer: File extensions help identify the type of a file and the application associated with it.

3. How can you determine the file type without relying on file extensions?

Answer: The file command in the Terminal can be used to identify file types based on their content.

Disk Management:

1. Explain the role of the /Volumes directory in macOS.

Answer:/Volumes is the default mount point for external volumes, including USB drives and network shares.

2. How can you check disk usage in macOS?

Answer: The df command provides information about disk space usage.

3. Describe the process of mounting and unmounting volumes in macOS.

Answer: Volumes can be mounted using the diskutil mount command and unmounted with diskutil unmount.

Backup and Recovery:

1. What backup solutions are available in macOS?

Answer: Time Machine is the built-in backup solution in macOS, and other options include third-party apps and cloud-based services.

2. How can you restore files using Time Machine?

Answer: Launch Time Machine, navigate to the desired date, and select "Restore" to recover files.

Command Line Operations:

1. How do you navigate the file system using the Terminal?

Answer: Use commands like cd to change directories and ls to list files.

2. Explain the purpose of the find command in macOS.

Answer: The find command is used to search for files and directories based on various criteria.

How can you create a symbolic link using the Terminal?

Answer: The ln -s command is used to create symbolic links.

System Integrity Protection (SIP):

1. What is System Integrity Protection (SIP) in macOS?

Answer:SIP is a security feature that restricts the modification of certain system files, even by administrators.

2. Can SIP be disabled, and if so, why might someone want to do that?

Answer:SIP can be disabled, but it's generally not recommended as it exposes the system to potential security risks.

Time Machine:

1. Explain the concept of snapshotting in Time Machine.

Answer: Time Machine uses snapshots to capture the state of the file system at specific points in time, allowing for efficient backups.

2. How can you exclude specific files or directories from Time Machine backups?

Answer: This can be done through the Time Machine preferences or by using the tmutil command in the Terminal.

Disk Utility:

1. What is the Disk Utility in macOS used for?

Answer: Disk Utility is a tool for managing disks and storage devices, including formatting, partitioning, and repairing.

2. Explain the process of creating a new partition using Disk Utility.

Answer: Open Disk Utility, select the disk, click on the "Partition" tab, and then click the "+" button to add a new partition.

Disk Encryption:

1. How does FileVault enhance security in macOS?

Answer: FileVault is a disk encryption program that protects data by encrypting the contents of the startup disk.

2. Can FileVault be turned on or off after the initial macOS setup?

Answer: Yes, FileVault can be enabled or disabled in the Security & Privacy preferences.

Spotlight Search:

1. What is Spotlight, and how does it enhance file system navigation?

Answer: Spotlight is a search feature that allows users to quickly locate files and applications on their Mac.

2. How can you customize Spotlight preferences to refine search results?

Answer: Go to System Preferences > Spotlight to adjust search categories and exclude certain folders.

File Compression and Archiving:

1. Explain the difference between zip and tar archive formats.

Answer: Zip is a compressed archive format, while tar is a file archiving format that may be compressed separately.

2. How can you create a compressed zip file in macOS?

Answer: Use the zip command in the Terminal, specifying the files or directories to include.

macOS Updates:

1. How are system updates managed in macOS?

Answer: Updates can be installed through the Software Update preference pane or using the softwareupdate command in the Terminal.

2. Can macOS updates be rolled back?

Answer: Generally, macOS updates are not designed to be rolled back. It's recommended to create backups before performing updates.

System Logs:

1. Where are system logs stored in macOS, and how can they be accessed?

Answer: System logs are stored in the /var/log directory, and they can be accessed using the log command or by viewing log files directly.

2. How can logs be helpful in troubleshooting file system issues?

Answer: Logs provide information about system events, errors, and warnings, aiding in the identification and resolution of issues.

Time Formats:

1. How does macOS represent file modification times?

Answer:macOS uses the Unix timestamp format to represent file modification times.

2. Can the file modification timestamp be manually modified?

Answer: Yes, the touch command can be used to change the modification timestamp of a file.

File System Monitoring:

1. Explain how the fseventsd process contributes to file system monitoring.

Answer:fseventsd is a daemon that monitors file system events, providing information for applications like Time Machine and Spotlight.

2. How can you monitor file system changes in real-time using the Terminal?

Answer: The fs_usage command can be used to display real-time file system activity, including reads, writes, and other events.

File Permissions and Ownership

Basic Concepts:

1. What are file permissions in macOS?

Answer: File permissions in macOS define who can read, write, or execute a file, and they are represented by the user (owner), group, and others.

2. Explain the significance of the three permission types: read, write, and execute.

Answer: Read allows viewing the file, write permits modification, and execute enables running a file as a program or script.

3. How are file ownership and file permissions related?

Answer: File ownership designates the user and group associated with a file, while file permissions determine the access rights for the owner, group, and others.

Command-Line Operations:

1. How can you view file permissions in the Terminal?

Answer: Use the ls -l command to display detailed file information, including permissions.

2. Describe the chmod command and its usage in changing file permissions.

Answer:chmod is used to change file permissions. For example, chmod +x filename grants execute permission.

3. Explain the purpose of the chown command.

Answer:chown is used to change the owner and/or group of a file. For instance, chown user: group filename changes ownership.

Ownership and Groups:

1. How can you determine the owner and group of a file in macOS?

Answer: Use the ls -l command to see the owner and group columns.

2. What is the difference between a user and a group in file ownership?

Answer:A user is an individual account, while a group is a collection of users. Files can be owned by a specific user and group.

3. How do you change the group ownership of a file?

Answer: Use the chown: newgroup filename command to change the group ownership.

Advanced Permissions:

1. Explain the purpose of the setuid, setgid, and sticky bit.

Answer: Setuid allows a program to run with the privileges of the file owner, setgid allows a program to run with the privileges of the group owner, and the sticky bit restricts file deletion in a directory.

2. How do you set the setuid permission on a file?

Answer: Use the chmod u+s filename command to set the setuid bit.

3. When would you use the sticky bit on a directory?

Answer: The sticky bit on a directory is commonly used on shared directories to prevent users from deleting files they don't own.

Default Permissions:

1. Where are default file permissions defined in macOS?

Answer: Default file permissions are often set by umask, which is a user-specific setting defined in the shell configuration files.

2. How can you change the default umask value?

Answer: The umask command is used to change the default umask value. For example, umask 022 sets the default permissions to 755 for directories and 644 for files.

Access Control Lists (ACLs):

1. What are Access Control Lists (ACLs) in macOS?

Answer:ACLs are an additional layer of permissions that allow more granular control over access to files and directories.

2. How can you view and modify ACLs in the Terminal?

Answer: Use the ls -le command to display ACLs and the chmod command with the "+" symbol to modify them.

3. **Provide an example of a situation where ACLs might be preferable to standard permissions.**

Answer:ACLs are useful when you need to grant specific permissions to a user or group without affecting the standard owner, group, and others permissions.

File Permission Troubleshooting:

1. How do you troubleshoot permission issues on a file or directory?

Answer: Check ownership, permissions, and ACLs using commands like ls -l and ls -le, and adjust them with chown and chmod as needed.

2. What is the significance of the "wheel" group in macOS?

Answer: The "wheel" group traditionally has elevated privileges and is often associated with administrative tasks.

Secure File Permissions:

1. Why is it important to set restrictive file permissions on sensitive files?

Answer: Restrictive permissions help prevent unauthorized access to sensitive information, reducing the risk of security breaches.

2. Can you enforce a policy where all files in a directory inherit specific permissions?

Answer: Yes, you can use the chmod command with the -R option to recursively set permissions for all files in a directory.

File Permissions and Networking:

1. How do file permissions interact with files accessed over a network in macOS?

Answer: File permissions are retained when files are transferred over a network. The user accessing the files needs the necessary permissions.

2. Explain how file permissions might impact file sharing among users.

Answer: File permissions determine which users can read, write, or execute files, impacting sharing and collaboration among users.

Time Machine and Permissions:

1. How does Time Machine handle file permissions during backup and restore?

Answer: Time Machine preserves file permissions during backup and restores them during a file restoration process.

2. Can you selectively restore files with different permissions using Time Machine?

Answer: Yes, Time Machine allows for selective file restoration, and restored files will retain their original permissions.

File Permissions and System Integrity Protection (SIP):

1. How does System Integrity Protection (SIP) impact file permissions in macOS?

Answer:SIP restricts modification of certain system files, enhancing security by limiting unauthorized changes.

2. Can SIP be temporarily disabled to modify protected system files?

Answer: It is generally not recommended to disable SIP, but it can be done temporarily for specific system modifications.

File Permissions Best Practices:

1. What are some best practices for managing file permissions on a macOS system?

Answer: Regularly audit and update permissions, limit access to sensitive files, and follow the principle of least privilege.

2. How do you ensure proper file permissions when transferring files between different systems?

Answer: Use consistent user and group names, set appropriate umask values, and validate permissions after transfers.

File Permissions and Backups:

1. How can you ensure that file permissions are preserved during file backups?

Answer: Use backup tools that support the preservation of file permissions, such as Time Machine.

2. In the context of backups, why is it important to consider both ownership and permissions?

Answer: Ownership and permissions are crucial for preserving the integrity of files during backup and ensuring they can be restored correctly.

Permissions and External Drives:

1. How does macOS handle file permissions on external drives?

Answer: Permissions on external drives are typically set to allow the user who mounts the drive full access.

2. Can file permissions on an external drive be different from the permissions on the main system drive?

Answer: Yes, permissions on external drives can be different and are usually managed independently.

File Permissions and Terminal Scripts:

1. How do file permissions impact the execution of shell scripts in the Terminal?

Answer: Execute permissions are required to run shell scripts. Ensure that the script file has the execute permission set.

2. How can you execute a script without modifying its file permissions?

Answer: Use the sh or bash command in the Terminal to execute a script without modifying its permissions.

Permissions and Software Installation:

1. Explain how file permissions might be affected during software installation in macOS.

Answer: Software installation can modify file permissions, particularly in system directories, to ensure proper functionality.

2. What precautions should be taken when installing software that requires elevated permissions?

Answer: Only install software from trusted sources, and be cautious when granting elevated permissions during the installation process.

Troubleshooting Ownership and Permissions:

1. Describe a scenario where a user is unable to access a file due to ownership and permission issues.

Answer: This could occur if the user does not have read permissions on the file or is not the owner.

2. How do you troubleshoot a situation where a user cannot modify a file despite having the write permission?

Answer: Check the ownership of the file. If the user is not the owner, they may need to modify the file as the owner or with administrative privileges.

Advanced Permissions and File Sharing:

1. In a shared directory, how can you ensure that new files created by different users have specific default permissions?

Answer: Set the umask appropriately for each user or use Access Control Lists (ACLs) to define default permissions for specific users or groups.

File Manipulation Commands

Basic File Manipulation:

1. How do you create an empty text file using the command line in macOS?

Answer: You can use the touch command, for example: touch filename.txt.

2. What command is used to copy files or directories in macOS?

Answer: The cp command is used for copying files and directories.

3. Explain the purpose of the mv command.

Answer: The mv command is used to move or rename files and directories.

Working with Directories:

1. How can you create a new directory using the command line?

Answer: The mkdir command is used to create a new directory, for example: mkdir new_directory.

2. What is the difference between the rmdir and rm -r commands in deleting directories?

Answer:rmdir is used to delete empty directories, while rm -r is used to delete directories and their contents recursively.

3. Explain the purpose of the cd command.

Answer: The cd command is used to change the current working directory.

Listing and Viewing Files:

1. How do you list the contents of a directory in macOS?

Answer: The ls command is used to list the contents of a directory.

2. What options can be used with the ls command to display detailed information about files?

Answer: The -l option provides detailed information, and -a shows hidden files as well.

3. How can you view the contents of a file without opening it?

Answer: The cat command can be used to display the contents of a file in the terminal.

File Removal:

1. Explain the difference between rm and rm -r.

Answer: rm is used to remove files, and rm -r is used to remove directories and their contents recursively.

2. How can you force the removal of a file or directory using the rm command?

Answer: The -f option can be added to the rm command to force removal without prompting.

3. What precaution should you take when using rm -rf?

Answer: Be cautious, as rm -rf will forcefully remove files and directories without confirmation, and data will be permanently deleted.

File Search and Find:

1. How can you search for files by name in macOS?

Answer: The find command, for example: find /path/to/search -name filename.txt.

2. What is the purpose of the grep command?

Answer: grep is used for searching text within files. For instance: grep "pattern" filename.txt.

3. How do you search for a file containing a specific text string in its content?

Answer: Use the grep command with the -r option, for example: grep -r "pattern" /path/to/search.

File Editing:

1. Which command-line text editor is pre-installed in macOS?

Answer: The nano text editor is available by default.

2. How can you open a file for editing using the nano editor?

Answer: Type nano filename.txt in the terminal to open the file for editing.

3. Explain the purpose of the sed command.

Answer: sed is a stream editor used for text manipulation, such as find and replace operations.

File Permissions:

1. How do you change file permissions using the chmod command?

Answer: Use the chmod command followed by the permission settings and the file name, for example: chmod 755 filename.txt.

2. What is the significance of the octal notation in file permissions?

Answer: Octal notation is a numerical representation of permissions (e.g., 755), where each digit corresponds to user, group, and other permissions.

3. How can you recursively change file permissions for a directory and its contents?

Answer: Use the -R option with the chmod command, for example: chmod -R 644 directory.

File Compression:

1. What command is used to create a compressed archive in macOS?

Answer: The tar command is often used, for example: tar -cvzf archive.tar.gz /path/to/directory.

2. How do you extract the contents of a compressed archive?

Answer: Use the tar -xvzf archive.tar.gz command to extract the contents.

3. Explain the purpose of the zip command.

Answer: The zip command is used to create and extract zip archives in macOS.

File System Navigation:

1. How do you navigate to the home directory using the command line?

Answer: The cd command followed by a tilde (~) will take you to the home directory, for example: cd ~.

2. What is the purpose of the pwd command?

Answer: The pwd command displays the current working directory.

3. How can you move up one level in the directory hierarchy using the command line?

Answer: Use the cd ..command to move up one level.

File System Information:

1. Explain the purpose of the df command.

Answer: The df command provides information about disk space usage and available space on mounted file systems.

2. How can you check the file system type of a particular volume?

Answer: Use the diskutil info /path/to/volume command to view information about a volume, including its file system type.

File System Maintenance:

1. What is the purpose of the diskutil command in macOS?

Answer:diskutil is a command-line utility for managing disks and volumes, including formatting, partitioning, and mounting.

2. How do you format a USB drive using the command line in macOS?

Answer: The diskutil eraseDisk command can be used, for example: diskutil eraseDisk ExFAT USB /dev/disk2.

File System Permissions and External Drives:

1. How are file permissions managed on external drives in macOS?

Answer: External drives are typically mounted with default permissions, allowing the user who mounts the drive full access.

2. Can you change file permissions on an external drive?

Answer: Yes, you can use the chmod command to modify file permissions on an external drive.

File Renaming and Moving:

1. How can you rename a file using the command line in macOS?

Answer: The mv command is used to rename a file, for example: mv oldname.txt newname.txt.

2. How do you move a file to a different directory using the mv command?

Answer: Use the mv command followed by the file name and the destination directory, for example: mv filename.txt /path/to/destination.

File System Monitoring:

1. What command can be used to monitor file system events in real-time?

Answer: The fs_usage command provides real-time information about file system activity.

2. How can you monitor changes to a specific file using the command line?

Answer: The fseventsd process and the fs_usage command can be used to monitor file system events related to a specific file.

File Permissions and Time Machine:

1. How does Time Machine handle file permissions during backup and restore?

Answer: Time Machine preserves file permissions during backup and restores them during a file restoration process.

2. Can you selectively restore files with different permissions using Time Machine?

Answer: Yes, Time Machine allows for selective file restoration, and restored files will retain their original permissions.

Secure File Manipulation:

1. What precautions should be taken when using file manipulation commands to ensure data integrity?

Answer: Verify commands before execution, back up important data, and be cautious with commands that can permanently delete files or directories.

Spotlight Search and Metadata

Spotlight Search Basics:

1. What is Spotlight Search in macOS?

Answer: Spotlight is a system-wide search feature that allows users to quickly locate files, applications, and other content on their Mac.

2. How can you initiate a Spotlight Search on macOS?

Answer: Press Command + Spacebar to open the Spotlight Search bar, or click the magnifying glass icon in the menu bar.

3. What types of content does Spotlight Search index by default?

Answer: Spotlight indexes files, applications, contacts, emails, calendar events, and more.

Customizing Spotlight Preferences:

1. How can you customize Spotlight preferences on macOS?

Answer: Go to System Preferences > Spotlight to adjust search categories, privacy settings, and keyboard shortcuts.

2. Explain the purpose of the Privacy tab in Spotlight preferences.

Answer: The Privacy tab allows users to exclude specific folders or volumes from Spotlight indexing.

3. Can you prioritize search results in Spotlight?

Answer: Yes, in Spotlight preferences, you can drag and drop categories to prioritize search results.

Metadata and Attributes:

1. What is metadata in the context of file systems?

Answer: Metadata includes additional information about files, such as file type, creation date, and author, without being part of the file content.

2. How does macOS store file metadata?

Answer:macOS uses extended attributes to store metadata, allowing for additional information beyond the traditional file attributes.

3. Can you modify file metadata in macOS?

Answer: Yes, metadata can be modified using commands like xattr or through third-party applications.

Advanced Spotlight Search:

1. Explain the use of boolean operators in Spotlight Search.

Answer: Boolean operators like AND, OR, and NOT can be used to refine searches. For example, searching for "photos NOT tagged" will exclude photos with tags.

2. How can you use Spotlight to perform calculations or unit conversions?

Answer: Type mathematical expressions or unit conversions directly into the Spotlight Search bar.

3. What role does natural language processing play in Spotlight Search?

Answer: Spotlight supports natural language queries, allowing users to search for files using everyday language.

Searching by File Types:

1. How can you filter search results in Spotlight to show only specific file types?

Answer: Use the file type operators such as "kind: image" to filter results to a specific type, like images.

2. Can you search for files created or modified within a specific timeframe using Spotlight?

Answer: Yes, use the "created:" and "modified:" operators, e.g., "created: yesterday" or "modified:1/1/2023."

3. Explain the purpose of the "kind:" operator in Spotlight Search.

Answer:"kind:" is used to filter results based on file types, such as documents, images, or applications.

Spotlight and System Preferences:

1. How can you exclude specific folders from being indexed by Spotlight?

Answer: Use the Privacy tab in Spotlight preferences to add folders or volumes that you want to exclude.

2. Can you disable Spotlight indexing altogether?

Answer: Yes, in Spotlight preferences, you can uncheck the checkbox for the volumes you want to exclude.

3. Explain the process of rebuilding the Spotlight index in macOS.

Answer: To rebuild the Spotlight index, go to System Preferences > Spotlight > Privacy, add your disk, then remove it. Spotlight will rebuild the index.

Spotlight and Accessibility:

1. How can Spotlight be beneficial for users with accessibility needs?

Answer: Spotlight provides a quick and efficient way for users with accessibility needs to navigate and locate files using the keyboard.

2. Can Spotlight be controlled using voice commands in macOS?

Answer: Yes, users can use Siri or voice commands to perform searches using Spotlight.

3. How does Spotlight assist in finding specific settings or preferences in System Preferences?

Answer: Typing keywords in the Spotlight Search bar can directly lead to specific settings or preferences within System Preferences.

Privacy and Security:

1. Are there privacy concerns associated with Spotlight Search?

Answer: Spotlight is designed with privacy in mind. However, users can exclude sensitive folders from indexing in Spotlight preferences.

2. How does macOS handle file permissions when indexing files for Spotlight?

Answer: Spotlight respects file permissions and only displays results that the user has permission to access.

3. Can Spotlight be used to search for content within encrypted files?

Answer: Spotlight can index and search within encrypted files, but the actual content remains encrypted.

Spotlight and iCloud:

1. How does Spotlight integrate with iCloud in macOS?

Answer: Spotlight can search for and display results from iCloud Drive, Mail, Contacts, Calendar, and other iCloud services.

2. Can Spotlight be used to find files stored in third-party cloud services?

Answer: Yes, third-party cloud services that integrate with Spotlight can be searched directly from the Spotlight Search bar.

Troubleshooting Spotlight Issues:

1. What steps would you take to troubleshoot Spotlight search issues?

Answer: Verify indexing preferences, rebuild the Spotlight index, and check for any conflicting third-party applications.

2. How can you check if Spotlight is currently indexing in macOS?

Answer: The Spotlight icon in the menu bar will have a dot in the middle while indexing. Alternatively, use the mdutil -s / command in the Terminal.

Automating Spotlight Searches:

1. Can Spotlight searches be automated in macOS?

Answer: Yes, AppleScript or Automator can be used to automate specific Spotlight searches and actions.

2. How would you create a custom Automator workflow for a specific Spotlight search?

Answer: Use Automator to create a workflow, add a "Spotlight Search" action, define search criteria, and add actions based on the results.

Time Machine and Spotlight:

1. How does Spotlight interact with Time Machine backups?

Answer: Spotlight indexes Time Machine backups, making it possible to search for and restore files from specific backup points.

2. Can you search for a specific file version using Spotlight and Time Machine?

Answer: Yes, Spotlight can show different versions of a file from Time Machine backups.

Collaboration and Spotlight:

1. How can Spotlight aid collaboration among users on a shared network?

Answer: Spotlight allows users to quickly find and access shared files on a network, enhancing collaboration.

2. Can you search for files owned by a specific user using Spotlight?

Answer: Yes, you can use the "owner:" operator to filter results based on file ownership.

Advanced Spotlight Commands:

1. What is the purpose of the mdfind command in macOS?

Answer:mdfind is a command-line utility that performs searches using the same metadata index as Spotlight.

2. How can you use the mdfind command to search for files modified within the last 24 hours?

Answer: Use the command mdfind "kMDItemDateAdded >= \$time.today(-1)" to find files modified in the last 24 hours.

System Integration:

1. How does Spotlight integrate with Siri in macOS?

Answer: Siri uses Spotlight's indexing to provide quick answers and actions based on natural language queries.

2. Can you search for and launch applications using Spotlight?

Answer: Yes, typing the name of an application in the Spotlight Search bar allows you to launch it quickly.

Future Developments:

1. Are there any recent or upcoming changes to Spotlight in the latest macOS versions?

Answer: Stay informed about the latest macOS updates and their impact on Spotlight by reviewing release notes and Apple documentation.

2. How would you envision the evolution of Spotlight Search in the next macOS versions?

Answer: Discuss potential improvements, integration with emerging technologies, and the ongoing relevance of Spotlight in enhancing user productivity.

ONLINE RESOURCES

Practice Paper Link: https://forms.gle/8mv2BWBgseE12ydZ8

QR Code:

Video Link: https://www.youtube.com/playlist?list=PLzlh_31VWEFq0ImTAlVGf-YHXLZo-XI6d

QR Code:

Chapter 4: mac OS Terminal and Shell Commands

Terminal Basics

Basic Commands:

1. How do you open the Terminal in macOS?

Answer: You can open the Terminal by navigating to Applications > Utilities > Terminal or by using the Spotlight Search (Command + Space and then typing "Terminal").

2. What is the purpose of the ls command in the Terminal?

Answer: The ls command is used to list the files and directories in the current directory.

3. How do you navigate to a different directory using the Terminal?

Answer: Use the cd command followed by the path of the directory you want to navigate to.

File and Directory Manipulation:

1. How can you create a new directory in the Terminal?

Answer: Use the mkdir command followed by the desired directory name, e.g., mkdir new_directory.

2. Explain the difference between the cp and mv commands.

Answer: The cp command is used to copy files or directories, while the mv command is used to move or rename them.

3. How do you remove a file in the Terminal?

Answer: Use the rm command followed by the filename, e.g., rm file.txt.

File Content Viewing and Editing:

1. What command is used to view the contents of a text file in the Terminal?

Answer: The cat command displays the entire contents of a file in the Terminal.

2. How can you view the contents of a large text file page by page?

Answer: The less command allows you to view the contents of a file page by page.

3. What is the purpose of the nano text editor?

Answer:nano is a simple text editor in the Terminal, used for viewing and editing text files.

Permissions and Ownership:

1. How can you view the permissions of a file in the Terminal?

Answer: Use the ls -l command to display detailed information, including permissions.

2. What is the significance of the symbols (r, w, x) in file permissions?

Answer: They represent read, write, and execute permissions for the owner, group, and others.

3. How do you change the owner of a file using the Terminal?

Answer: The chown command is used to change the owner, e.g., chown newowner filename.txt.

Advanced Commands:

1. What does the ps command do in the Terminal?

Answer: The ps command is used to display information about active processes.

2. How do you find a file or directory in the Terminal?

Answer: Use the find command, e.g., find /path/to/search -name filename.txt.

3. Explain the purpose of the grep command.

Answer:grep is used for searching text within files or command output.

System Information:

1. What does the uname command display in the Terminal?

Answer:uname displays system information, including the system name and version.

2. How can you check the available disk space in the Terminal?

Answer: Use the df command to display disk space information.

3. What is the purpose of the top command?

Answer:top displays real-time information about system processes and resource usage.

Command History and Shortcuts:

1. How can you repeat the last command in the Terminal?

Answer: Press !!or use the history command to find the command number and then type !n to repeat the nth command.

2. Explain the significance of the Ctrl + C shortcut in the Terminal.

Answer: Ctrl + Cis used to interrupt or terminate a running command.

3. How can you clear the Terminal screen?

Answer: Use the clear command or press Command + K to clear the Terminal screen.

Environment Variables:

1. What is the purpose of environment variables in the Terminal?

Answer: Environment variables store information about the system environment and user preferences.

2. How do you display the value of an environment variable?

Answer: Use echo $VARIABLE_NAME to display the value of the specified environment variable.

3. How can you set a new environment variable in the Terminal?

Answer: Use the export command, e.g., export VARIABLE_NAME=value.

Networking Commands:

1. How do you check your network connection in the Terminal?

Answer: Use the ping command followed by a website or IP address.

2. What command displays information about network interfaces?

Answer: The ifconfig command provides information about network interfaces.

3. How can you retrieve information about a domain's DNS records in the Terminal?

Answer: Use the dig command, e.g., dig example.com.

Scripting and Automation:

1. What scripting language is commonly used in macOS Terminal?

Answer: Bash (Bourne Again SHell) is the default scripting language in macOS Terminal.

2. How can you make a script executable in the Terminal?

Answer: Use the chmod +x script.sh command to make a script executable.

3. What is the purpose of the #!/bin/bash shebang line in a script?

Answer: It specifies the path to the Bash interpreter, indicating that the script should be executed using Bash.

Text Manipulation:

1. How can you count the number of lines in a text file in the Terminal?

Answer: Use the wc -l command, e.g., wc -l filename.txt.

2. What command can be used to sort lines in a text file alphabetically?

Answer: The sort command, e.g., sort filename.txt.

3. How do you find and replace text in a file using the Terminal?

Answer: Use the sed command for find and replace operations, e.g., sed 's/old/new/g' filename.txt.

System Maintenance:

1. How can you update the package list on macOS using the Terminal?

Answer: Use the sudo software update -i -a command to update the package list.

2. What is the purpose of the sudo command in the Terminal?

Answer:sudo is used to execute commands with elevated privileges.

3. How can you shut down or restart the system from the Terminal?

Answer: Use the sudo shutdown -h now command to shut down or sudo shutdown -r now to restart.

Package Management:

1. What package management system is used in macOS?

Answer:macOS uses the brew (Homebrew) package manager for installing and managing software.

2. How do you install a package using Homebrew in the Terminal?

Answer: Use the brew install package_name command, e.g., brew install wget.

3. How can you uninstall a package using Homebrew?

Answer: The brew uninstall package_name command removes a package, e.g., brew uninstall wget.

User and Group Management:

1. How do you add a new user in the Terminal?

Answer: Use the sudo dscl . -create /Users/username command to add a new user.

Command-Line Navigation

Basic Navigation:

1. How do you display the current working directory in the Terminal?

Answer: Use the pwd command to print the current working directory.

2. What command is used to change the current directory in the Terminal?

Answer: The cd command is used to change the current directory.

3. How can you list the contents of a directory in the Terminal?

Answer: Use the ls command to list files and directories in the current location.

Advanced Navigation:

1. Explain the use of the ls -l command in the Terminal.

Answer:ls -l provides a detailed list view, showing file permissions, ownership, size, and modification time.

2. How do you navigate to the home directory in the Terminal?

Answer: Use the command cd ~ to navigate to the home directory.

3. What does the cd ..command do?

Answer:cd ..moves up one level in the directory hierarchy.

Path Handling:

1. How do you navigate to a directory with a space in its name?

Answer: Enclose the directory name in quotes, e.g., cd "My Documents".

2. Explain the significance of the .and ..entries in directory listings.

Answer:.refers to the current directory, and ..refers to the parent directory.

3. How can you navigate to a specific directory using an absolute path?

Answer: Use the cd /full/path/to/directory command to navigate using an absolute path.

Wildcards and Globbing:

1. What does the * wildcard represent in the Terminal?

Answer: The * wildcard matches any sequence of characters.

2. How can you list all files with a specific extension using wildcards?

Answer: Use the ls *.extension command, e.g., ls *.txt to list all text files.

3. Explain the purpose of the ?wildcard in command-line navigation.

Answer: The ?wildcard matches any single character.

File and Directory Creation:

1. How do you create a new directory in the Terminal?

Answer: Use the mkdir command followed by the desired directory name, e.g., mkdir new_directory.

2. What command is used to create an empty text file in the Terminal?

Answer: The touch command is used to create empty files, e.g., touch filename.txt.

3. How can you create a directory and its parent directories in one command?

Answer: Use the -p option with mkdir, e.g., mkdir -p parent_directory/new_directory.

Copying and Moving:

1. How do you copy a file from one location to another in the Terminal?

Answer: Use the cp command, e.g., cp file.txt /path/to/destination.

2. What is the purpose of the -r option in the cp command?

Answer: The -r option is used to copy directories and their contents recursively.

3. How do you move a file to a different location in the Terminal?

Answer: Use the mv command, e.g., mv file.txt /path/to/destination.

File and Directory Removal:

1. What command is used to remove a file in the Terminal?

Answer: The rm command is used to remove files, e.g., rm filename.txt.

2. How can you remove a directory and its contents in the Terminal?

Answer: Use the rm -r command, e.g., rm -r directory.

3. Explain the purpose of the -i option in the rm command.

Answer: The -i option prompts for confirmation before removing each file.

Searching for Files:

1. How do you search for a file by name in the Terminal?

Answer: Use the find command, e.g., find /path/to/search -name filename.txt.

2. What is the purpose of the grep command in file searching?

Answer:grep is used for searching text within files, e.g., grep "pattern" filename.txt.

3. How can you search for files modified within the last 24 hours?

Answer: Use the find command with the -mtime option, e.g., find /path/to/search -mtime -1.

File Viewing and Editing:

1. How do you view the contents of a text file in the Terminal?

Answer: Use commands like cat, less, or more, e.g., cat filename.txt.

2. What command is used to edit a text file in the Terminal?

Answer: You can use text editors like nano, vim, or emacs, e.g., nano filename.txt.

3. How can you search for text within a file while viewing it in the Terminal?

Answer: In commands like less or more, type /pattern to search for text within the file.

File Permissions and Ownership:

1. How do you view the permissions of a file in the Terminal?

Answer: Use the ls -lcommand, and the permissions will be displayed in the first column.

2. How can you change the permissions of a file in the Terminal?

Answer: Use the chmod command, e.g., chmod 644 filename.txt to set read and write permissions for the owner.

3. What command is used to change the owner of a file in the Terminal?

Answer: The chown command is used to change the owner, e.g., chown newowner filename.txt.

File Compression and Decompression:

1. How can you create a compressed archive in the Terminal?

Answer: Use the tar command, e.g., tar -czvf archive.tar.gz /path/to/directory.

2. What command is used to decompress a tar.gz archive?

Answer: Use the tar -xzvf archive.tar.gz command to decompress the contents.

3. Explain the purpose of the zip command in the Terminal.

Answer: The zip command is used to create and extract zip archives.

Terminal Shortcuts and History:

1. How can you recall the previous command without retyping it?

Answer: Press the Up Arrow key to cycle through previous commands.

2. What is the purpose of the Ctrl + R shortcut in the Terminal?

Answer: Ctrl + Rinitiates a reverse search in command history.

3. How do you repeat the last argument of the previous command?

Answer: Use the !!:$ syntax, e.g., cp file.txt /path/to/destination/ !!:$ to repeat the last argument.

System Information:

1. How can you check the system's uptime in the Terminal?

Answer: Use the uptime command to display the system's uptime.

2. What command provides detailed information about system hardware?

Answer: The system_profiler command displays detailed system information.

3. How can you retrieve information about available disk space?

Answer: Use the df -h command to display disk space information in a human-readable format.

Networking Commands:

1. How can you check if a remote server is reachable from the Terminal?

Answer: Use the ping command followed by the server's IP address or domain name.

Essential Shell Commands

Basic Commands:

1. How do you open a new Terminal window in macOS?

Answer: You can open a new Terminal window by pressing Command + N or by selecting "New Window" from the "Shell" menu.

2. What is the purpose of the echo command in the shell?

Answer: The echo command is used to display text or variables in the Terminal.

3. How can you check the version of the shell in use?

Answer: Use the echo $SHELL command to display the path of the current shell.

Environment Variables:

1. What are environment variables, and why are they important in the shell?

Answer: Environment variables store information about the system environment and user preferences, influencing how commands behave.

2. How can you set a new environment variable in the shell?

Answer: Use the export command, e.g., export VARIABLE_NAME=value.

3. Explain the significance of the $PATH environment variable.

Answer:$PATH defines the directories where the shell looks for executable files, allowing you to run commands without specifying the full path.

File and Directory Manipulation:

1. How do you list the contents of a directory in the shell?

Answer: The ls command is used to list files and directories in the current location.

2. What is the purpose of the pwd command?

Answer: The pwd command prints the current working directory.

3. How can you create a new directory in the shell?

Answer: Use the mkdir command followed by the desired directory name, e.g., mkdir new_directory.

File Operations:

1. How do you copy a file from one location to another in the shell?

Answer: Use the cp command, e.g., cp file.txt /path/to/destination.

2. What command is used to move a file or directory?

Answer: The mv command is used to move or rename files and directories, e.g., mv oldname.txt newname.txt.

3.How do you remove a file in the shell?

Answer: Use the rm command, e.g., rm filename.txt.

File Viewing and Editing:

1. What command is used to display the contents of a text file in the shell?

Answer: Commands like cat, less, or more can be used, e.g., cat filename.txt.

2. How can you edit a text file in the shell?

Answer: Use text editors like nano, vim, or emacs, e.g., nano filename.txt.

3. Explain the purpose of the head and tail commands.

Answer:head displays the first part of a file, and tail displays the last part.

File Permissions and Ownership:

1. How do you view the permissions of a file in the shell?

Answer: Use the ls -l command to display detailed information, including permissions.

2. How can you change the permissions of a file in the shell?

Answer: Use the chmod command, e.g., chmod 644 filename.txt to set read and write permissions for the owner.

3. What command is used to change the owner of a file in the shell?

Answer: The chown command is used to change the owner, e.g., chown newowner filename.txt.

Directory Navigation:

1. How do you change the current directory in the shell?

Answer: Use the cd command followed by the path of the directory you want to navigate to.

2. What is the purpose of the ..entry in directory listings?

Answer:..refers to the parent directory.

3. How can you navigate to your home directory in the shell?

Answer: Use the cd ~ command to navigate to the home directory.

Wildcards and Globbing:

1. What does the * wildcard represent in the shell?

Answer: The * wildcard matches any sequence of characters.

2. How can you list all files with a specific extension using wildcards?

Answer: Use the ls *.extension command, e.g., ls *.txt to list all text files.

3. Explain the purpose of the ?wildcard in shell commands.

Answer: The ?wildcard matches any single character.

System Information:

1. How can you check the system's uptime in the shell?

Answer: Use the uptime command to display the system's uptime.

2. What command provides detailed information about system hardware?

Answer: The system_profiler command displays detailed system information.

3. How can you retrieve information about available disk space?

Answer: Use the df -h command to display disk space information in a human-readable format.

Networking Commands:

1. How can you check if a remote server is reachable from the shell?

Answer: Use the ping command followed by the server's IP address or domain name.

2. What command displays information about network interfaces?

Answer: The ifconfig command provides information about network interfaces.

3. How can you retrieve information about a domain's DNS records in the shell?

Answer: Use the dig command, e.g., dig example.com.

Process Management:

1. What command is used to display information about active processes?

Answer: The ps command provides information about active processes.

2. How do you terminate a running process in the shell?

Answer: Use the kill command followed by the process ID, e.g., kill PID.

3. What does the top command do in the shell?

Answer:top displays real-time information about system processes and resource usage.

File Compression and Decompression:

1. How can you create a compressed archive in the shell?

Answer: Use the tar command, e.g., tar -czvf archive.tar.gz /path/to/directory.

2. What command is used to decompress a tar.gz archive?

Answer: Use the tar -xzvf archive.tar.gz command to decompress the contents.

3. Explain the purpose of the zip command in the shell.

Answer: The zip command is used to create and extract zip archives.

Shortcuts and History:

1. How can you recall the previous command without retyping it?

Answer: Press the Up Arrow key to cycle through previous commands.

2. What is the purpose of the Ctrl + C shortcut in the shell?

Answer: Ctrl + Cis used to interrupt or terminate a running command.

3. How do you search for a command in your command history?

Answer: Use Ctrl + R to initiate a reverse search in command history.

System Maintenance:

1. How can you update the package list on macOS using the shell?

Answer: Use the sudo softwareupdate -i -a command to update the package list.

ONLINE RESOURCES

Practice Paper Link: https://forms.gle/vynZZhuRPRKD8xQy6

QR Code:

Video Link: https://www.youtube.com/playlist?list=PLzlh_31VWEFoCHKXDCKJ7c6vn8tefsfQN

QR Code:

Chapter 5: mac OS App Management

Installing and Removing Applications

Application Installation:

1. How do you install applications on macOS?

Answer: On macOS, applications can be installed using various methods, including the Mac App Store, direct downloads from the internet, or package managers like Homebrew.

2. What is the Mac App Store, and how does it simplify application installation?

Answer: The Mac App Store is Apple's official platform for distributing macOS applications. It simplifies installation by providing a centralized location for users to discover, purchase, and install applications with a single click.

3. Explain the process of installing an application downloaded from the internet.

Answer: After downloading the application, typically in a .dmg or .pkg file, you mount the disk image (if applicable), drag the application to the Applications folder, and complete any additional setup steps.

Homebrew Package Manager:

1. What is Homebrew, and how does it facilitate application management on macOS?

Answer: Homebrew is a popular package manager for macOS that simplifies the installation and management of command-line tools and applications. It provides a convenient way to install, update, and remove software.

2. How do you install Homebrew on a macOS system?

Answer: Open Terminal and run the command /bin/bash -c "$(curl -fsSL https://raw.githubusercontent.com/Homebrew/install/master/install.sh)". This installs Homebrew.

3. Can you provide an example of installing a package using Homebrew?

Answer: Certainly, brew install package_name installs the specified package. For instance, brew install wget installs the wget tool.

Command-Line Installation:

1. How can you install applications using the command line on macOS?

Answer: The installer command can be used to install packages from the command line. For example, sudo installer -pkg PackageName.pkg -target /.

2. What is the purpose of the sudo command in the context of application installation?

Answer:sudo is used to execute commands with elevated privileges, necessary for installing system-level applications or modifying certain directories.

Application Removal:

1. How do you uninstall an application on macOS?

Answer: Applications can be uninstalled by dragging them to the Trash. Additionally, some applications provide uninstallers, and others can be removed using third-party uninstaller tools.

2. Can you explain the significance of the uninstall command in application removal?

Answer: The uninstall command is often provided by application developers to remove their software and associated files completely. It's an alternative to manual removal.

3. What precautions should be taken before uninstalling an application?

Answer: Before uninstalling, it's advisable to check for associated files in directories like ~/Library/Application Support/ and ~/Library/Preferences/. Additionally, some applications may leave behind configuration files.

Troubleshooting Installations:

1. How do you troubleshoot installation issues on macOS?

Answer: Common troubleshooting steps include checking system logs, verifying system requirements, ensuring proper permissions, and searching for solutions on support forums.

2. What is the purpose of the Console application in troubleshooting installations?

Answer: The Console app provides access to system logs, helping diagnose errors and issues during installation. It can be found in Applications > Utilities > Console.

3. Can you explain the role of the system_profiler command in troubleshooting?

Answer:system_profiler provides detailed information about system hardware and software, aiding in diagnosing compatibility issues during installations.

Updates and Upgrades:

1. How do you update applications on macOS?

Answer: Updates for applications from the Mac App Store are typically managed through the App Store app. For other applications, updates may be handled within the application itself or via the developer's website.

2. What is the purpose of the softwareupdate command in macOS?

Answer: The softwareupdate command allows users to install system updates and, optionally, updates for other software installed on the system.

3. How can you check for available updates using Homebrew?

Answer:brew update updates Homebrew, and brew outdated lists outdated packages. To update, use brew upgrade.

App Store and System Preferences:

1. Where can you manage App Store preferences on macOS?

Answer: App Store preferences are managed in the "App Store" pane within the "System Preferences" application.

2. How can you enable automatic updates for applications from the Mac App Store?

Answer: In "System Preferences," go to "App Store," and check the option for "Automatically check for updates" and "Download newly available updates in the background."

3. Explain the significance of the "Allow apps downloaded from" setting in System Preferences > Security & Privacy.

Answer: This setting controls the sources from which apps can be installed. It can be set to "App Store," "App Store and identified developers," or "Anywhere."

Application Security:

1. How can you verify the authenticity of an application before installation?

Answer: Check for digital signatures or certificates, download from official sources or app stores, and read reviews. Gatekeeper in macOS can help verify signed applications.

2. What is Gatekeeper, and how does it enhance application security?

Answer: Gatekeeper is a security feature that helps protect your Mac by controlling what software is allowed to run. It verifies the digital signature of applications to ensure they come from trusted sources.

3. How can you check the code signature of an application using Terminal?

Answer: Use the codesign -dv --verbose=4 /path/to/application.app command to check the code signature.

Disk Space Management:

1. How can you check the available disk space on your Mac?

Answer: The df -h command in Terminal provides a human-readable summary of disk space usage.

2. What steps can be taken to free up disk space on a Mac?

Answer: Delete unnecessary files, empty the Trash, use the "Optimize Storage" feature, and consider removing large applications or moving files to external storage.

Application Preferences and Settings:

1. Where are application preferences stored on macOS?

Answer: Application preferences are often stored in the ~/Library/Preferences/ directory.

2. How can you reset an application to its default settings?

Answer: Deleting the preference file associated with the application in the ~/Library/Preferences/ directory often resets an application to its default settings.

Automation and Scripting:

1. How can you automate the installation of multiple applications on macOS?

Answer: Scripting tools like Bash or using configuration management tools like Ansible can automate the installation of multiple applications.

2. Can you provide an example of a shell script that installs multiple applications?

Answer: Certainly, a script might use commands like brew install or download and install applications directly from the internet.

Application Licensing:

1. How do you handle software licensing when installing applications on multiple Macs?

Answer: It depends on the licensing terms. Some applications require a separate license for each installation, while others allow multiple installations within a specified organization.

2. What considerations should be taken into account when managing licenses for enterprise-level applications?

Answer: Enterprise-level applications may require a centralized license server, adherence to license agreements, and proper documentation for compliance.

Application Dependencies:

1. How do you manage dependencies when installing applications with Homebrew?

Answer: Homebrew automatically resolves and installs dependencies when installing a package. Dependencies are managed by Homebrew itself.

2. Can you explain the concept of runtime libraries and their importance in application installation?

Answer: Runtime libraries are shared libraries that applications depend on to run. Ensuring the availability of required runtime libraries is crucial for successful application installation.

Application Logs:

1. Where are application logs typically stored on macOS?

Answer: Application logs are often found in the ~/Library/Logs/ directory.

2. How can you view real-time logs for an application in Terminal?

Answer: Use the tail -f ~/Library/Logs/ApplicationName.log command to view real-time logs for a specific application.

App Store Connect:

1. What is App Store Connect, and how is it relevant to application developers?

Answer: App Store Connect is a web-based platform that allows developers to manage and distribute their apps on the App Store. It provides tools for app submission, analytics, and financial reporting.

2. How can you submit a new application to the App Store as a developer?

Answer: Developers submit applications through Xcode, Apple's integrated development environment, following the guidelines outlined in the App Store Connect portal.

Application Compatibility:

1. How do you determine if an application is compatible with a specific version of macOS?

Answer: Check the application's official website or documentation for system requirements and compatibility information. Developers often provide this information.

2. What steps can be taken to run older applications on a newer version of macOS?

Answer: Try running the application in compatibility mode, check for updates from the developer, or consider using virtualization or emulation solutions.

3. How can you check for and install updates for non-App Store applications?

Answer: Some applications have built-in update mechanisms. For others, visit the developer's website or use package managers like Homebrew to check for updates.

App Store Usage

General App Store Usage:

1. How do you access the App Store on macOS?

Answer: The App Store can be accessed from the Apple menu or the Dock. Alternatively, you can open it directly from the Applications folder.

2. What types of applications are available on the Mac App Store?

Answer: The Mac App Store offers a wide range of applications, including productivity tools, utilities, games, and multimedia apps.

3. How do you search for a specific application in the App Store?

Answer: Use the search bar in the top-right corner of the App Store and enter the name of the application.

App Store Account and Preferences:

1. Where can you manage your App Store account settings on macOS?

Answer: App Store account settings are managed in the "App Store" pane within the "System Preferences" application.

2. How can you view your purchase history on the Mac App Store?

Answer: In the App Store, go to your account by clicking on your name in the bottom-left corner, then select "View Information," and scroll down to "Purchase History."

3. Explain the purpose of the "Updates" tab in the App Store.

Answer: The "Updates" tab displays available updates for installed applications, including system updates.

App Installation and Management:

1. How do you install an application from the Mac App Store?

Answer: Click on the "Get" or "Price" button next to the app, and then click "Install." You may need to sign in with your Apple ID.

2. Can you install applications from sources other than the Mac App Store on macOS?

Answer: Yes, applications can be installed from sources other than the Mac App Store. This includes direct downloads from the internet or installations using package managers like Homebrew.

3. How do you update applications installed from the Mac App Store?

Answer: Open the App Store, go to the "Updates" tab, and click the "Update" button next to each app with available updates.

In-App Purchases and Subscriptions:

1. What are in-app purchases, and how do they work on macOS?

Answer: In-app purchases are additional content or features that can be bought within an application. They are managed through the App Store, and users can make purchases using their Apple ID.

2. How can you manage subscriptions for applications on macOS?

Answer: In the App Store, go to your account, select "View Information," then scroll down to "Manage" next to Subscriptions.

3. What considerations should be taken into account when implementing in-app purchases in a macOS application?

Answer: Developers should follow Apple's guidelines, provide clear information about purchases, and ensure a smooth user experience.

App Store Security:

1. How does Apple ensure the security of applications on the Mac App Store?

Answer: Apple reviews applications before they are made available on the App Store, checking for compliance with guidelines, security, and performance.

2. What is Gatekeeper, and how does it enhance security in App Store apps?

Answer: Gatekeeper is a security feature that verifies the digital signature of applications, ensuring they come from trusted sources. This helps prevent the installation of malicious software.

3. Can you explain the significance of app notarization in the context of App Store apps?

Answer: App notarization is a process where Apple checks an app for malicious content. Notarized apps have an extra layer of security.

App Ratings and Reviews:

1. How do users submit ratings and reviews for applications on the Mac App Store?

Answer: Users can leave ratings and reviews by going to the App Store, finding the app, and clicking on the "Ratings & Reviews" section.

2. What steps can developers take to encourage positive reviews for their applications?

Answer: Provide excellent customer support, regularly update the app, and encourage users to leave reviews without incentivizing or manipulating feedback.

App Store Guidelines and Compliance:

1. What are the App Store Review Guidelines, and why are they important for developers?

Answer: The guidelines outline the rules developers must follow for their apps to be accepted on the App Store. Adherence ensures a consistent and high-quality user experience.

2. Can you provide an example of a situation where an app might violate App Store guidelines?

Answer: Apps that contain inappropriate content, violate user privacy, or engage in deceptive practices could violate guidelines.

3. How can developers appeal a decision made by the App Store review team?

Answer: Developers can submit an appeal through the App Store Connect website if they believe a decision was made in error.

Family Sharing and App Store Policies:

1. What is Family Sharing, and how does it work on the Mac App Store?

Answer: Family Sharing allows family members to share purchased apps, music, and more. It requires setting up a Family Sharing group and sharing the same payment method.

2. How does Apple handle refund requests for App Store purchases?

Answer: Apple may issue refunds for app purchases in certain situations, and users can request a refund through the "Report a Problem" feature in the App Store.

3. What is the role of the "Ask to Buy" feature in Family Sharing?

Answer:"Ask to Buy" allows parents to approve or decline app purchases initiated by children in their Family Sharing group.

App Analytics and Reporting:

1. How can developers access analytics for their applications on the App Store?

Answer: Developers can access detailed analytics through the App Store Connect website, providing insights into app performance, user engagement, and more.

2. What types of data are available in App Store Connect analytics?

Answer: Developers can access data on app downloads, user engagement, sales, crash reports, and other metrics.

3. How can developers use analytics data to improve their applications?

Answer: Analyzing user behavior, identifying popular features, and addressing performance issues are ways developers can use analytics to enhance their apps.

App Store Connect for Developers:

1. What is App Store Connect, and how does it benefit developers?

Answer: App Store Connect is a web-based platform that allows developers to manage their apps on the App Store. It provides tools for app submission, analytics, and financial reporting.

2. How can developers submit a new application to the Mac App Store?

Answer: Developers use Xcode to submit their apps to the App Store. This involves preparing the app, creating an App Store Connect record, and following the submission process.

3. What steps should developers take to prepare their apps for submission to the Mac App Store?

Answer: Follow Apple's App Store guidelines, test thoroughly, provide accurate metadata, and ensure the app adheres to user interface guidelines.

App Store Updates:

1. How does the App Store handle updates for installed applications?

Answer: Users receive notifications about available updates, and they can manually update apps through the App Store.

2. Can you explain the concept of "app thinning" in the context of App Store updates?

Answer: App thinning is the process of delivering only the necessary components of an app for a specific device, reducing download sizes and optimizing storage usage.

3. What considerations should be taken into account when releasing major updates for an application on the App Store?

Answer: Communicate changes to users, test thoroughly to avoid bugs, and consider user feedback for ongoing improvements.

Developer Relations:

1. How can developers communicate with Apple regarding issues or questions related to the App Store?

Answer: Developers can use the "Contact Us" option in the App Store Connect website or engage with Apple Developer Support.

2. What resources are available for developers to stay informed about App Store updates and changes?

Answer: Apple provides developer documentation, release notes, and updates through the Apple Developer website and App Store Connect.

App Store Optimization:

1. What is App Store Optimization (ASO), and why is it important for developers?

Answer: ASO involves optimizing app metadata (title, keywords, description) to improve visibility and discoverability on the App Store, ultimately increasing downloads.

2. How can developers optimize their app listings for better visibility in the App Store?

Answer: Use relevant keywords, create compelling app descriptions, provide high-quality visuals, and encourage positive reviews.

Mac Catalyst and Universal Apps:

1. What is Mac Catalyst, and how does it impact the development of apps for macOS?

Answer: Mac Catalyst allows developers to bring iPad apps to the Mac with minimal modification, providing a consistent user experience across platforms.

2. How can developers create universal apps that run on both macOS and iOS?

Answer: Developers can use frameworks like SwiftUI and UIKit to create apps that adapt to different screen sizes and input methods, ensuring a seamless experience on both macOS and iOS.

App Store Trends:

1. How can developers stay informed about current trends and user preferences on the App Store?

Answer: Monitoring user reviews, analysing app analytics, and staying engaged with the developer community are ways developers can stay informed about trends.

2. Can you provide an example of an app that successfully leveraged App Store trends for its success?

Answer: Apps that respond to emerging needs or leverage new technologies often gain traction. For example, apps that embraced augmented reality or health and fitness trends.

Software Updates and Upgrades

Software Update Basics:

1. How can users check for software updates on macOS?

Answer: Users can check for updates in the "Software Update" section of the "System Preferences."

2. What is the purpose of the "Automatically keep my Mac up to date" option in Software Update preferences?

Answer: This option enables automatic downloading and installation of system updates to keep the macOS system up to date.

3. How does the macOS update process differ for App Store applications and system software?

Answer: App Store applications are updated through the App Store, while system software updates are managed in the "Software Update" section of "System Preferences."

Command-Line Updates:

1. How can you check for software updates using the Terminal?

Answer: Use the command softwareupdate -l to list available updates, and sudo softwareupdate -i -a to install them.

2. Explain the purpose of the --install and --ignore options in the softwareupdate command.

Answer:--install is used to install specific updates, and --ignore is used to exclude certain updates from being installed.

3. What steps should be taken before initiating a command-line software update?

Answer: Ensure you have administrative privileges (sudo), and back up critical data to avoid potential data loss during the update.

App Store Application Updates:

1. How can users update applications downloaded from the Mac App Store?

Answer: Open the App Store, go to the "Updates" tab, and click the "Update" button next to each app with available updates.

2. What is the significance of the "Update All" button in the App Store for application updates?

Answer: The "Update All" button allows users to update all applications with available updates simultaneously.

3. Can users enable automatic updates for applications downloaded from the Mac App Store?

Answer: Yes, in "System Preferences," under "App Store," users can enable "Automatically check for updates" and "Download newly available updates in the background."

Software Update Preferences:

1. Where are the software update preferences located in macOS?

Answer: Software update preferences can be found in the "System Preferences" under the "Software Update" section.

2. How can users customize the frequency of software update checks in macOS?

Answer: Users can set the frequency of checks in the "Advanced" section of "Software Update" preferences.

3. Explain the purpose of the "Download new updates when available" option in software update preferences.

Answer: This option allows macOS to download available updates in the background, making the installation process faster.

macOS Version Upgrades:

1. What is the process for upgrading to a new major macOS version?

Answer: Major macOS upgrades are typically available through the Mac App Store. Users can find and download the upgrade from the "Updates" tab.

2. How can users check if their Mac is eligible for a macOS version upgrade?

Answer: Check the system requirements for the new macOS version on the Apple website or the Mac App Store.

3. What precautions should users take before upgrading to a new macOS version?

Answer: Back up important data, check application compatibility, and ensure the Mac meets the system requirements for the new version.

macOS Beta Updates:

1. What is the macOS Beta Program, and how can users participate?

Answer: The macOS Beta Program allows users to test pre-release versions of macOS. Users can enroll their Mac in the program through the Apple Beta Software Program website.

2. What considerations should users be aware of when using beta versions of macOS?

Answer: Beta versions may contain bugs and compatibility issues. It's recommended to test on a secondary device and not on a primary, critical system.

3. How can users provide feedback on beta versions of macOS?

Answer: Users can use the Feedback Assistant app to report bugs and provide feedback directly to Apple.

Troubleshooting Updates:

1. What steps can users take if a macOS update fails to install?

Answer: Restart the Mac, check for sufficient disk space, and ensure a stable internet connection. If the issue persists, check system logs for error messages.

2. How can users roll back or uninstall a macOS update if issues arise?

Answer: Rolling back updates can be challenging. The best approach is to restore from a Time Machine backup taken before the problematic update.

3. Explain the role of Safe Mode in troubleshooting update issues.

Answer: Booting into Safe Mode can help diagnose and resolve issues by starting up with a minimal set of drivers and preventing certain software from loading.

Software Update Logs:

1. Where can users find logs related to software updates in macOS?

Answer: Software update logs are available in the Console app under "Logs" > "Install.log."

2. How can users interpret error messages in software update logs?

Answer: Error messages in logs provide insights into why an update may have failed. They often include specific error codes and descriptions.

App Store Connect and Deployment:

1. What is the role of App Store Connect in managing software updates for developers?

Answer: App Store Connect allows developers to submit, manage, and distribute updates for their applications on the App Store.

2. How can developers schedule the release of updates for their applications on the App Store?

Answer: Developers can use App Store Connect to schedule the release date and time for app updates.

3. What considerations should developers keep in mind when submitting updates to the App Store?

Answer: Follow Apple's guidelines, test thoroughly, provide accurate metadata, and ensure the app adheres to user interface guidelines.

Software Update Automation:

1. How can system administrators automate software updates on multiple Macs?

Answer: Tools like Apple Remote Desktop or configuration management systems can be used to automate and manage software updates across multiple Macs.

2. What are the advantages and challenges of automating software updates in a corporate environment?

Answer: Automation ensures timely updates, but challenges include compatibility testing, potential disruptions, and the need for careful planning.

Security Updates:

1. Why are security updates important, and how often should they be installed?

Answer: Security updates address vulnerabilities and should be installed promptly. The frequency depends on the release schedule from Apple.

2. Can users prioritize the installation of security updates over other updates?

Answer: Security updates are typically prioritized and installed automatically. Users can ensure this by enabling automatic updates.

3. What steps can users take to verify the authenticity of security updates?

Answer: Download updates only from the official Apple website or through the built-in Software Update feature.

Custom Software Repositories:

1. How can organizations set up custom software repositories for managing updates?

Answer: Organizations can use tools like Reposado or create a local Apple Software Update server to manage and distribute updates internally.

2. What are the advantages of using custom software repositories for updates in an enterprise environment?

Answer: Custom repositories provide control over update distribution, bandwidth optimization, and the ability to test updates before deployment.

Update Rollouts:

1. How can developers roll out updates gradually to a subset of users on the App Store?

Answer: Developers can use phased releases in App Store Connect to gradually release updates to users over a set period.

2. What are the benefits of a phased release strategy for updates?

Answer: Phased releases allow developers to monitor for issues, gather feedback, and ensure a smooth rollout to all users.

App Store Connect Analytics:

1. How can developers use App Store Connect analytics to track the performance of app updates?

Answer: App Store Connect provides detailed analytics on app updates, including download numbers, user engagement, and more.

2. What metrics are valuable for developers to analyze in App Store Connect after releasing an update?

Answer: Key metrics include adoption rates, crash reports, user reviews, and user engagement data.

Compatibility Testing:

1. How can developers ensure their applications remain compatible with new macOS versions?

Answer: Developers should participate in beta testing, regularly test their apps on pre-release macOS versions, and stay informed about changes in developer documentation.

2. Can you provide an example of a situation where an application update might lead to compatibility issues?

Answer: Changes in system APIs, deprecated features, or modifications in security policies can lead to compatibility issues with app updates.

ONLINE RESOURCES

Practice Paper Link: https://forms.gle/CB7Q3mqjZro74BmG9

QR Code:

Video Link: https://www.youtube.com/playlist?list=PLzlh_31VWEFq9GyFdTzTdIQYw8Yh39CEF

QR Code:

Chapter 6: mac OS Security Features

User Authentication

General Concepts:

1. What is user authentication, and why is it crucial in operating systems?

Answer: User authentication is the process of verifying the identity of a user. It is critical for security, ensuring that only authorized users can access a system or its resources.

2. Explain the difference between authentication and authorization.

Answer: Authentication verifies the identity of a user, while authorization determines the permissions and access level granted to that authenticated user.

3. What role does user authentication play in securing macOS systems?

Answer: User authentication is the first line of defense in preventing unauthorized access to macOS systems, safeguarding user data and system resources.

Password-Based Authentication:

1. How are user passwords stored on macOS for local accounts?

Answer: Passwords are securely hashed and stored using a one-way hashing algorithm in the /etc/shadow file.

2. Can you explain the purpose of the Keychain Access application in macOS?

Answer: Keychain Access manages passwords, encryption keys, and certificates, providing a secure storage solution for user credentials.

3. What measures can be taken to enhance the security of password-based authentication?

Answer: Implementing strong password policies, enabling multi-factor authentication (MFA), and regularly updating passwords contribute to enhanced security.

Multi-Factor Authentication (MFA):

1. How does multi-factor authentication (MFA) enhance user authentication security?

Answer:MFA requires users to provide multiple forms of identification (e.g., password and a token), adding an extra layer of security beyond just a password.

2. What MFA options are available on macOS?

Answer:macOS supports various MFA methods, including Apple ID two-factor authentication, third-party authenticator apps, and hardware tokens.

3. Can you explain the workflow of Apple ID two-factor authentication on macOS?

Answer: After entering the password, a second factor (usually sent to a trusted device) is required to complete the login process.

Biometric Authentication:

1. What biometric authentication features are available on macOS?

Answer:macOS supports Touch ID and Face ID on supported hardware for quick and secure biometric authentication.

2. How does biometric authentication enhance user convenience and security?

Answer: Biometric authentication provides a convenient and secure way for users to access their devices without relying solely on passwords.

Directory Services and Authentication:

1. What is the role of Directory Services in user authentication on macOS?

Answer: Directory Services manages user and system configuration information, including user authentication details, within a network directory.

2. Can macOS authenticate users against multiple directory services?

Answer: Yes, macOS can authenticate users against various directory services, including Open Directory, LDAP, and Active Directory.

Single Sign-On (SSO):

1. What is Single Sign-On (SSO), and how does it benefit users?

Answer:SSO allows users to log in once and gain access to multiple applications or services without re-entering credentials, enhancing user convenience.

2. How is Single Sign-On implemented on macOS?

Answer:macOS supports SSO through technologies like Kerberos, which allows users to authenticate once and access various services seamlessly.

Kerberos Authentication:

1. What is Kerberos, and how does it facilitate user authentication on macOS?

Answer: Kerberos is a network authentication protocol that enables secure communication over an untrusted network, commonly used for single sign-on.

2. Can you explain the Kerberos ticket-granting ticket (TGT) and service ticket in the authentication process?

Answer: The TGT is obtained during initial authentication and is used to request service tickets. Service tickets grant access to specific services.

Open Directory:

1. What is Open Directory, and how is it used for user authentication on macOS?

Answer: Open Directory is Apple's implementation of a directory service, supporting user authentication and centralized user management.

2. How can administrators configure Open Directory on macOS for user authentication?

Answer: Open Directory can be configured through the "Directory Utility" in "System Preferences" to connect to an LDAP or Active Directory server.

LDAP Authentication:

1. How does Lightweight Directory Access Protocol (LDAP) contribute to user authentication on macOS?

Answer:macOS can use LDAP to authenticate users against a central directory service, enabling a single point of authentication for multiple systems.

2. What considerations should be taken into account when configuring macOS for LDAP authentication?

Answer: Ensure secure communication by using LDAP over SSL (LDAPS), configure appropriate authentication settings, and test connectivity.

Active Directory Integration:

1. Can macOS authenticate users against Microsoft Active Directory?

Answer: Yes, macOS can integrate with Active Directory, allowing users to log in using their AD credentials.

2. What tools and utilities are available on macOS for configuring Active Directory integration?

Answer: The "Directory Utility" in "System Preferences" and the dsconfigad command-line tool are used to configure Active Directory integration.

Authentication Authorization and Accounting (AAA):

1. What is Authentication, Authorization, and Accounting (AAA), and how is it relevant to user authentication?

Answer:AAA is a framework for controlling access to network resources. Authentication verifies identity, authorization determines access, and accounting tracks resource usage.

2. How can AAA principles be applied in macOS environments?

Answer:AAA principles are applied through the configuration of access controls, user permissions, and logging mechanisms on macOS systems.

Smart Card Authentication:

1. How does smart card authentication work on macOS?

Answer: Smart cards contain cryptographic information that, when used with a compatible reader, allows users to authenticate securely.

2. What are the advantages of smart card authentication in enterprise environments?

Answer: Smart card authentication enhances security by requiring a physical card and a PIN, making unauthorized access more difficult.

Secure Tokens and FileVault:

1. What is a secure token in the context of user authentication on macOS?

Answer:A secure token is a credential that allows a user to unlock and access the FileVault-encrypted startup disk on a Mac.

How is FileVault related to user authentication, and how does it use secure tokens?

Answer: FileVault uses secure tokens to enable users to unlock their encrypted startup disk during the login process.

Account Management:

1. What steps can administrators take to manage user accounts securely on macOS?

Answer: Enforce strong password policies, regularly review and update user accounts, and promptly disable accounts for departed users.

2. Can you explain the significance of role-based access control (RBAC) in user authentication?

Answer:RBAC assigns roles and permissions based on job responsibilities, ensuring users have access only to the resources necessary for their roles.

Password Policies:

1. How can administrators enforce strong password policies on macOS?

Answer: Configure password policies using "System Preferences" or enforce policies through a directory service like Open Directory or Active Directory.

2. What elements should be considered when creating an effective password policy?

Answer: Consider password length, complexity requirements, expiration intervals, and account lockout policies to enhance security.

User Account Lockout:

1. Why is user account lockout important, and how can it be configured on macOS?

Answer: Account lockout helps prevent brute-force attacks. macOS allows administrators to configure account lockout settings in "System Preferences."

2. What should administrators consider when determining the threshold for account lockout attempts?

Answer: Balance security with user convenience, setting a threshold that mitigates brute-force attacks without causing inconvenience for users.

Remote Authentication:

1. How does remote authentication work on macOS, especially in the context of SSH or VPN access?

Answer:macOS supports remote authentication through protocols like SSH and VPN, where users can authenticate using passwords, keys, or other methods.

2. What security considerations should be taken into account when implementing remote authentication?

Answer: Use secure protocols, implement encryption, and consider additional security measures such as two-factor authentication for remote access.

Token-Based Authentication:

1. How does token-based authentication work, and what advantages does it offer on macOS?

Answer: Token-based authentication involves the use of cryptographic tokens, enhancing security by requiring possession of a physical device.

2. Can you provide an example of a situation where token-based authentication might be preferable over other methods?

Answer: Token-based authentication is often preferred in high-security environments, such as government or finance, where an additional layer of physical security is necessary.

Biometric Data Security:

1. How is biometric data stored and secured on macOS devices?

Answer: Biometric data, such as fingerprints or facial features, is securely stored in the Secure Enclave on supported Mac hardware, and it is never directly accessible or stored by applications.

File Permissions and Security

File Permissions Basics:

1. What are file permissions, and why are they important on macOS?

Answer: File permissions define who can access a file, and what actions (read, write, execute) can be performed. They are crucial for securing data and system files.

2. How are file permissions represented in the macOS terminal?

Answer: File permissions are represented as a series of characters, such as -rwxr-xr--, where each character indicates the permission for the owner, group, and others.

3. Can you explain the significance of the three permission sets: owner, group, and others?

Answer: The owner is the user who owns the file, the group is a collection of users, and others refer to everyone else. File permissions are set independently for each of these sets.

Changing File Permissions:

1. How can you change file permissions in the macOS terminal?

Answer: Use the chmod command, followed by the desired permission settings and the file name.

2. Describe the meaning of the numeric representation of file permissions (e.g., 755).

Answer: The numeric representation condenses file permissions, where each digit corresponds to the owner, group, and others, respectively, using octal values.

3. What is the significance of the chown command in macOS, and how is it used?

Answer: The chown command changes the owner of a file. It is used as chown [new_owner] [file].

File Ownership:

1. How can you identify the owner and group of a file in the macOS terminal?

Answer: Use the ls -l command, and the owner and group will be listed in the file details.

2. What is the difference between the chown and chgrp commands?

Answer:chown changes the file owner, while chgrp changes the file group.

3. How can you recursively change the ownership of a directory and its contents?

Answer: Use the -R option with the chown command: chown -R [new_owner] [directory].

File Permissions and Security:

1. Why is it important to carefully manage file permissions on a macOS system?

Answer: Proper file permissions enhance system security by ensuring that only authorized users or processes can access, modify, or execute specific files.

2. What is the significance of the sticky bit in file permissions?

Answer: The sticky bit, when applied to a directory, restricts the deletion of files within that directory to the file owner. It is denoted by a 't' in the permissions.

3. How does macOS handle the execution of scripts and applications with file permissions?

Answer:macOS uses the "Gatekeeper" security feature to verify and control the execution of scripts and applications, checking for digital signatures.

Access Control Lists (ACLs):

1. What are Access Control Lists (ACLs) in the context of file permissions?

Answer:ACLs provide a more granular level of control over file permissions, allowing users to define specific permissions for multiple users or groups.

2. How can you view the ACLs of a file in the macOS terminal?

Answer: Use the ls -le command to display extended attributes and ACL information.

3. Can you provide an example of a situation where using ACLs might be preferable over standard file permissions?

Answer:ACLs are useful when more detailed control is needed, such as granting specific users or groups different levels of access to a file or directory.

File System Encryption:

1. What is FileVault, and how does it contribute to file system security on macOS?

Answer: FileVault is a disk encryption program in macOS that uses XTS-AES-128 encryption with a 256-bit key to help prevent unauthorized access to information on startup disks.

2. How can users enable or disable FileVault on their macOS system?

Answer: FileVault can be enabled/disabled in "System Preferences" under "Security & Privacy" > "FileVault."

Secure File Deletion:

1. How can you securely delete a file in macOS to prevent recovery?

Answer: Use the srm (secure remove) command or the shred command to securely delete files, overwriting the data to make it more difficult to recover.

2. Why is secure file deletion important, especially for sensitive information?

Answer: Secure file deletion helps prevent unauthorized recovery of sensitive data, ensuring that deleted files cannot be easily accessed by malicious actors.

File Permissions in Networked Environments:

1. How do file permissions work when files are accessed over a network on macOS?

Answer: File permissions are enforced based on the user credentials provided during the network connection. The user's permissions on the remote system are applied.

2. What is the significance of the umask command in the context of file permissions?

Answer:umask sets the default permissions for newly created files and directories, ensuring a consistent permission scheme.

Security Considerations for Shared Directories:

1. How can administrators set up shared directories on macOS with proper security measures?

Answer: Use the "Sharing" preferences in "System Preferences" to configure shared folders, and apply appropriate file permissions to limit access.

2. What precautions should be taken when sharing files between users on a macOS system?

Answer: Use shared directories with appropriate permissions, limit access to necessary users, and regularly review and update permissions.

Network File Systems (NFS) Security:

1. How does macOS handle security in Network File System (NFS) environments?

Answer:macOS supports NFS and enforces file permissions based on the user credentials provided during the NFS connection.

2. What security measures should be implemented for secure NFS file sharing on macOS?

Answer: Use the nfsd daemon for NFS file sharing, configure proper file permissions, and consider using the krb5 security mechanism for encrypted NFS traffic.

File Permissions Auditing:

1. Why is it important to audit file permissions on a macOS system?

Answer: File permissions auditing helps ensure compliance with security policies, identifies potential security risks, and allows administrators to take corrective actions.

2. What tools are available on macOS for auditing file permissions?

Answer: Use the ls command with various options (-l, -la, -le) for basic auditing. For more advanced auditing, consider third-party tools or scripts.

Time Machine and File Permissions:

1. How does Time Machine handle file permissions when creating backups?

Answer: Time Machine preserves file permissions and metadata, ensuring that restored files maintain the same security settings as the original files.

2. Can users selectively restore files with specific permissions from a Time Machine backup?

Answer: Users can restore individual files or directories from a Time Machine backup, and the original file permissions will be retained.

SIP (System Integrity Protection):

1. What is System Integrity Protection (SIP), and how does it impact file permissions on macOS?

Answer:SIP protects system files and directories from being modified, even by the root user, ensuring the integrity of the operating system.

2. Can SIP be disabled, and what are the implications of doing so?

Answer:SIP can be disabled, but it is not recommended as it exposes the system to potential security vulnerabilities. Disabling SIP requires booting into recovery mode.

Application Sandboxing:

1. How does application sandboxing contribute to file security on macOS?

Answer: Sandboxed applications run in restricted environments, limiting their access to the file system and enhancing overall system security.

2. What considerations should developers keep in mind when implementing sandboxing for macOS applications?

Answer: Developers should carefully define the application's entitlements, minimize file system access to only what is necessary, and regularly update their app's security settings.

Gatekeeper and Code Signing:

1. What is Gatekeeper, and how does it enhance file security on macOS?

Answer: Gatekeeper is a security feature that checks the code signature of applications, ensuring they are from identified developers and have not been altered.

2. How can developers sign their applications to comply with Gatekeeper requirements?

Answer: Developers sign applications using their Apple Developer ID, and the apps are distributed through the Mac App Store or other trusted channels.

XProtect and File Security:

1. What is XProtect, and how does it contribute to file security on macOS?

Answer:XProtect is an anti-malware feature that scans downloaded files for known malicious content, protecting the system from common threats.

2. How frequently is XProtect updated, and can users manually update its definitions?

Answer:XProtect definitions are regularly updated by Apple. Users cannot manually update definitions but can ensure automatic updates are enabled.

File Permissions Troubleshooting:

1. What steps can be taken to troubleshoot file permission issues on a macOS system?

Answer: Check file ownership and permissions using the ls and chmod commands, review system logs for errors, and use the Disk Utility for disk-related issues.

How can the "Repair Disk Permissions" feature in Disk Utility be used to address file permission issues?

Answer: Disk Utility's "Repair Disk Permissions" feature checks and corrects file permissions on system files. However, this feature is deprecated in recent macOS versions.

Security Best Practices:

What are some best practices for maintaining secure file permissions on macOS?

Answer: Enforce the principle of least privilege, regularly audit file permissions, use encryption for sensitive data, keep the system and applications updated, and follow Apple's security guidelines.

Firewall and Privacy Settings

Firewall Basics:

1. What is a firewall, and how does it enhance security on macOS?

Answer:A firewall is a network security system that monitors and controls incoming and outgoing network traffic. On macOS, it helps protect the system by regulating communication with external networks.

2. How can you enable or disable the built-in firewall on macOS?

Answer: The built-in firewall on macOS can be enabled or disabled in "System Preferences" under "Security & Privacy" > "Firewall."

3. What are the two modes of the macOS firewall, and how do they differ?

Answer: The macOS firewall has two modes: "Allow all incoming connections" and "Block all incoming connections." The former allows all incoming connections, while the latter blocks all incoming connections.

Application Firewall:

1. Explain the difference between the network firewall and the application firewall on macOS.

Answer: The network firewall controls overall network traffic, while the application firewall specifically regulates the network activity of individual applications.

2. How can users configure the application firewall to control specific app access?

Answer: Users can configure the application firewall in "Security & Privacy" settings, under the "Firewall" tab, by clicking "Firewall Options" and selecting specific applications.

3. What role does the "Stealth Mode" option play in the macOS application firewall?

Answer: Stealth Mode prevents the system from responding to probing requests, adding an extra layer of security by making the system less visible to potential attackers.

Network Ports and Services:

1. How can users view and manage open network ports on macOS?

Answer: The lsof command can be used to view open network ports, and the firewall settings can be configured to control access to specific ports.

2. Can you explain the concept of port forwarding and how it relates to firewall settings?

Answer: Port forwarding redirects network traffic from one port to another, often used to allow external access to specific services. Firewall settings can be configured to allow or block port forwarding.

3. What security considerations should be taken into account when configuring port forwarding on a macOS system?

Answer: Minimize the number of open ports, use strong authentication methods, and regularly review and update port forwarding rules to prevent unauthorized access.

Stealth and Security:

1. How does the "Stealth Mode" in the application firewall contribute to system security?

Answer: Stealth Mode makes the system less discoverable by not responding to unauthorized probing requests, providing an additional layer of security against potential attackers.

2. Can enabling "Stealth Mode" impact the functionality of certain network services or applications?

Answer: Yes, certain network services or applications may rely on the system responding to probing requests. Enabling "Stealth Mode" may affect their functionality.

3. What measures can be taken to balance security and functionality when using "Stealth Mode"?

Answer: Customize "Stealth Mode" settings to allow necessary services while still limiting responses to unauthorized probing requests. Regularly review and update these settings.

Firewall Logging:

1. How can administrators view firewall logs on macOS?

Answer: Firewall logs can be accessed in the Console app under "Logs" > "Firewall.log."

2. What information can be found in firewall logs, and how is it useful for security monitoring?

Answer: Firewall logs contain information about blocked or allowed connections, providing insights into potential security threats and helping administrators monitor network activity.

3. How can the logging level of the macOS firewall be adjusted?

Answer: The logging level can be adjusted using the defaults write command in the terminal. For example, sudo defaults write /Library/Preferences/com.apple.alf logging_level 2 sets the logging level to 2.

Privacy Settings:

1. What privacy settings are available in macOS, and how do they enhance user privacy?

Answer: Privacy settings include controls over location services, microphone access, camera access, contacts, and more. They enhance user privacy by allowing granular control over which apps can access sensitive data.

2. How can users manage app permissions for privacy settings on macOS?

Answer: Users can manage app permissions in "System Preferences" under "Security & Privacy" > "Privacy." There, they can control access to various sensitive data types.

3. What considerations should be taken into account when allowing or denying app permissions for privacy settings?

Answer: Users should carefully review and understand why an app is requesting specific permissions. Denying unnecessary permissions enhances privacy and security.

Location Services:

1. How does the Location Services feature in macOS contribute to user privacy?

Answer: Location Services allow apps to use location-based information. Users can control which apps have access to this data in "Security & Privacy" settings.

2. Can users enable or disable Location Services for specific apps?

Answer: Yes, users can enable or disable Location Services for specific apps in "System Preferences" under "Security & Privacy" > "Privacy" > "Location Services."

3. What security implications should users be aware of when using Location Services?

Answer: Enabling Location Services may expose location data to apps. Users should only grant this access to trusted apps and review app permissions regularly.

Microphone and Camera Access:

1. How can users manage microphone and camera access for applications on macOS?

Answer: Users can manage these settings in "System Preferences" under "Security & Privacy" > "Privacy" > "Microphone" and "Camera."

2. What are the security concerns associated with granting microphone and camera access to apps?

Answer: Granting unnecessary access may compromise user privacy. Users should be cautious and only grant access to trusted apps with a legitimate need for these features.

3. Can users receive notifications when an app accesses the microphone or camera?

Answer: Yes, users can receive notifications by enabling the "Show a notification when an app accesses the microphone" and "Show a notification when an app accesses the camera" options in privacy settings.

Contacts and Calendars:

1. How does macOS handle privacy settings related to contacts and calendars?

Answer: Users can control which apps have access to contacts and calendars in "Security & Privacy" settings under the "Privacy" tab.

2. Why is it important to review and manage app permissions for contacts and calendars?

Answer: Granting unnecessary access to contacts and calendars may expose sensitive information. Regularly reviewing and managing app permissions enhances privacy and security.

Full Disk Access:

1. What is Full Disk Access, and how can users configure it for enhanced privacy?

Answer: Full Disk Access grants apps access to all files on the system. Users can manage this setting in "Security & Privacy" under "Privacy" > "Full Disk Access."

2. What precautions should users take when granting Full Disk Access to applications?

Answer: Users should carefully review and understand why an app is requesting Full Disk Access. Only grant this access to trusted apps with a legitimate need for such access.

Safari Privacy Settings:

1. How can users enhance privacy in Safari on macOS?

Answer: Users can configure privacy settings in Safari, including blocking cross-site tracking, preventing camera and microphone access, and managing website data.

2. What is Intelligent Tracking Prevention (ITP), and how does it contribute to user privacy in Safari?

Answer:ITP is a feature in Safari that blocks third-party cookies and prevents cross-site tracking, enhancing user privacy while browsing.

3. How can users manage website data and cookies in Safari for improved privacy?

Answer: Users can manage website data and cookies in Safari preferences under the "Privacy" tab. They can block all cookies, allow from current website only, or allow from visited websites.

Gatekeeper and App Privacy:

1. How does Gatekeeper contribute to app privacy on macOS?

Answer: Gatekeeper ensures that apps come from identified developers and have not been tampered with, enhancing app security and user privacy.

2. Can users adjust Gatekeeper settings to allow apps from different sources?

Answer: Yes, users can adjust Gatekeeper settings in "Security & Privacy" under "General" to allow apps from the App Store or identified developers, or from anywhere (with caution).

iCloud Privacy Settings:

1. How does iCloud handle user privacy settings on macOS?

Answer: Users can manage iCloud privacy settings in "System Preferences" under "Apple ID" > "iCloud," controlling which apps and services can access and store data in iCloud.

2. What considerations should users keep in mind when syncing data with iCloud for privacy?

Answer: Users should be aware of the types of data being synced with iCloud and consider disabling syncing for sensitive information if not necessary.

FileVault and Disk Encryption:

1. How does FileVault contribute to user privacy on macOS?

Answer: FileVault encrypts the startup disk, ensuring that data is secure even if the physical disk is removed from the device.

2. Can users enable or disable FileVault after the initial macOS setup?

Answer: Yes, users can enable or disable FileVault at any time in "System Preferences" under "Security & Privacy" > "FileVault."

Privacy Concerns with Third-Party Apps:

1. What privacy considerations should users keep in mind when using third-party apps on macOS?

Answer: Users should review app permissions, only install apps from trusted sources, and be cautious about granting unnecessary access to sensitive data.

2. Can users manage privacy settings for third-party apps on macOS similar to system apps?

Answer: Yes, users can manage privacy settings for third-party apps in "Security & Privacy" settings under the "Privacy" tab.

System Integrity Protection (SIP):

1. What is System Integrity Protection (SIP), and how does it contribute to user privacy on macOS?

Answer:SIP protects critical system files and directories from modification, ensuring the integrity of the operating system and enhancing overall system security and privacy.

ONLINE RESOURCES

Practice Paper Link: https://forms.gle/zs2BqhysM9476TubA

QR Code :

Video Link: https://www.youtube.com/playlist?list=PLzlh_31VWEFoz2P0J7n1-OkrkmdQuYJ_j

QR Code :

Chapter 7: mac OS Applications and Utilities

Key mac OS Applications

Finder and System Preferences:

1. Explain the role of Finder in macOS, and what are some essential features?

Answer: Finder is the file management application in macOS. It allows users to browse, organize, and manipulate files and folders. Essential features include file navigation, searching, and file management.

2. How can users customize Finder preferences for an optimized file management experience?

Answer: Users can customize Finder preferences in "Finder" > "Preferences," adjusting settings such as default folder views, sidebar items, and search options.

3. What key settings can be configured in macOS System Preferences, and how does it impact the user experience?

Answer: System Preferences is the central hub for configuring system settings. Users can customize display, sound, network, and security settings to tailor the macOS experience to their preferences.

Safari Web Browser:

1. What features distinguish Safari as the default web browser on macOS?

Answer: Safari is known for its speed, energy efficiency, and integration with macOS features. It includes features like Reader mode, Intelligent Tracking Prevention, and privacy settings.

2. How can users manage bookmarks and reading lists in Safari?

Answer: Users can add, organize, and edit bookmarks in the bookmarks bar. Reading lists allow users to save articles for later reading and sync across devices.

3. Explain the role of Safari Extensions and how users can manage them.

Answer: Safari Extensions enhance the browser's functionality. Users can manage extensions in Safari preferences under the "Extensions" tab, enabling or disabling them as needed.

Mail Application:

1. What are some key features of the Mail application on macOS?

Answer: The Mail app allows users to manage multiple email accounts, organize emails with folders, use Smart Mailboxes, and integrate with other macOS applications.

2. How can users set up and configure multiple email accounts in the Mail app?

Answer: Users can add email accounts in "Mail" > "Preferences" > "Accounts" by providing account details, including the incoming and outgoing server information.

3. Explain how Smart Mailboxes work and how users can benefit from them.

Answer: Smart Mailboxes are virtual mailboxes that automatically organize emails based on criteria. Users can create them for specific contacts, subjects, or keywords for efficient email management.

Calendar and Reminders:

1. What functionalities does the Calendar app offer, and how can users manage multiple calendars?

Answer: The Calendar app allows users to schedule events, set reminders, and manage multiple calendars. Users can color-code calendars and sync them across devices.

2. How can users create and manage reminders in the Reminders app?

Answer: Users can create reminders in the Reminders app and organize them into lists. Reminders can be set for specific times, locations, or based on arrival/departure.

3. Explain how the Calendar and Reminders apps integrate with other macOS applications and services.

Answer: Calendar and Reminders integrate with Siri, allowing users to create events and reminders using voice commands. They also sync with iCloud for cross-device access.

Contacts and FaceTime:

1. What features does the Contacts app offer, and how can users manage contact information?

Answer: The Contacts app allows users to store and organize contact information, sync with other applications, and use the information in various macOS features.

2. How can users initiate and manage FaceTime calls on macOS?

Answer: Users can initiate FaceTime calls through the Contacts app or directly from the FaceTime app. Calls can include video or audio, and users can create favorites for quick access.

3. Explain the integration of Contacts and FaceTime with other Apple devices.

Answer: Contacts and FaceTime information syncs across Apple devices using iCloud, providing a seamless experience for users across their devices.

Messages and iMessage:

1. What are the key features of the Messages app on macOS?

Answer: Messages allows users to send and receive text messages, photos, videos, and more. It also supports iMessage, which includes features like read receipts and end-to-end encryption.

2. How can users use iMessage features such as effects and Animoji on macOS?

Answer: Users can add effects to messages by selecting the "Effects" button. Animoji and Memoji can be added to messages with supported Mac models.

3. Explain how the Messages app integrates with the Messages app on iOS devices.

Answer: Messages syncs across macOS and iOS devices using iCloud. Users can start a conversation on one device and continue it on another seamlessly.

Photos and Preview:

1. What functionalities does the Photos app provide for managing and editing photos on macOS?

Answer: The Photos app allows users to organize, edit, and share photos. It includes features like facial recognition, Memories, and integration with iCloud Photos.

2. How can users edit and enhance photos using the editing tools in the Photos app?

Answer: Users can access editing tools in the Photos app to adjust exposure, color balance, and add filters. Advanced editing options include cropping, rotating, and retouching.

3. Explain the role of the Preview app in macOS and its key functionalities.

Answer: Preview is a versatile app for viewing and annotating documents and images. It supports various file formats and allows users to add annotations, signatures, and more.

Pages, Numbers, and Keynote:

1. What is the purpose of the Pages app, and how does it differ from traditional word processors?

Answer: Pages is a word processing app that combines powerful features with a user-friendly interface. It allows users to create documents with rich formatting and media.

2. How does the Numbers app contribute to spreadsheet creation and data analysis on macOS?

Answer: Numbers is a spreadsheet application that provides tools for creating and editing spreadsheets. It includes features like charts, formulas, and collaborative editing.

3. Explain the role of the Keynote app and its advantages for creating presentations.

Answer: Keynote is a presentation app that enables users to create visually stunning slideshows. It offers templates, animations, and collaboration features for engaging presentations.

iMovie and GarageBand:

1. What capabilities does iMovie offer for video editing on macOS?

Answer:iMovie is a video editing app that allows users to create and edit videos with ease. It includes features for adding transitions, effects, and soundtracks.

2. How can users create and edit music using GarageBand on macOS?

Answer: GarageBand is a digital audio workstation that allows users to create and edit music. It includes virtual instruments, audio effects, and support for third-party plugins.

Maps and Apple Maps:

1. What features does the Maps app offer on macOS, and how does it integrate with other applications?

Answer: The Maps app provides directions, points of interest, and real-time traffic information. It integrates with other apps, allowing users to plan routes and share locations.

2. How can users use Apple Maps to navigate and explore locations on macOS?

Answer: Users can enter destinations in Apple Maps to get directions, view 3D maps, and explore points of interest. It also provides real-time traffic information and transit directions.

Time Machine and Backup:

1. Explain the purpose of Time Machine on macOS and how users can set up backups.

Answer: Time Machine is a backup feature that automatically backs up the entire system. Users can set up backups using an external drive, and it provides easy recovery of files or the entire system.

2. How can users restore files or the entire system using Time Machine?

Answer: Users can enter Time Machine and navigate through snapshots to find and restore specific files. For a complete system restore, macOS can be reinstalled using Time Machine.

Preview and Markup:

1. How can users use the Markup tools in Preview to annotate and edit documents?

Answer: Users can open a document in Preview, click the "Markup" button, and use tools like text, shapes, and signatures to annotate and edit the document.

2. Explain how Preview integrates with other applications for document viewing and editing.

Answer: Preview is the default application for viewing PDFs and images. It integrates with other apps, providing quick access to viewing and annotating documents.

Terminal and Command-Line Tools:

1. What role does the Terminal play in macOS, and how can users benefit from command-line tools?

Answer: Terminal is a command-line interface that allows users to interact with the Unix-based core of macOS. Command-line tools provide powerful options for system administration and automation.

2. Can you provide examples of essential command-line tools and their use cases in macOS?

Answer: Examples include ls for listing files, cp for copying files, mv for moving files, and grep for searching within files. These tools are fundamental for system management and troubleshooting.

Preview and Accessibility:

1. How can users leverage accessibility features in macOS for improved user experience?

Answer:macOS includes accessibility features like VoiceOver, Magnifier, and Display accommodations. Users can customize these features in "System Preferences" under "Accessibility."

2. Explain the role of Preview in supporting accessibility features for document viewing.

Answer: Preview supports accessibility features such as VoiceOver, allowing users with visual impairments to navigate and interact with documents.

App Store and Software Updates:

1. How can users discover, download, and install applications using the App Store on macOS?

Answer: Users can access the App Store, browse categories, search for apps, and click "Get" to download and install them. Purchased apps are tied to the user's Apple ID.

2. How are software updates managed on macOS, and why is it important to keep the system updated?

Answer: Software updates can be installed through "System Preferences" > "Software Update." Keeping the system updated is crucial for security, bug fixes, and accessing new features.

Contacts and Integration with Mail:

1. How does the Contacts app integrate with the Mail app to enhance communication?

Answer: Contacts provides a centralized location for managing contact information. When integrated with Mail, it allows for easy access to email addresses and contact details when composing messages.

2. Can users sync Contacts with external accounts such as Google or Microsoft for cross-platform access?

Answer: Yes, users can sync Contacts with external accounts in "System Preferences" > "Internet Accounts," enabling seamless access to contacts across multiple platforms.

Utility Tools for Productivity

Spotlight and Siri:

1. How does Spotlight enhance productivity on macOS, and what are some advanced search features?

Answer: Spotlight is a system-wide search tool. Advanced features include file type filters, calculations, and natural language queries to quickly locate files, apps, and information.

2. How can users customize Spotlight preferences to optimize search results?

Answer: Users can customize Spotlight preferences in "System Preferences" > "Spotlight," choosing which categories to include in search results and adjusting the order.

3. Explain the integration of Siri into macOS and its productivity features.

Answer: Siri on macOS allows users to perform tasks using voice commands, such as sending messages, setting reminders, and searching the web, enhancing hands-free productivity.

Automator and Workflow Automation:

1. What is Automator, and how can users create workflows for repetitive tasks?

Answer: Automator is a visual scripting tool that allows users to automate tasks by creating workflows. Users can chain together actions to perform complex operations with a single click.

2. Provide examples of productivity workflows that can be created using Automator.

Answer: Workflows can include renaming batches of files, resizing images, converting file formats, and automating repetitive actions across multiple applications.

3. How does Automator integrate with other macOS applications and system services?

Answer: Automator integrates with various applications, allowing users to create custom actions for specific apps. It also interacts with system services for broader automation capabilities.

Terminal and Shell Scripting:

1. How can the Terminal and shell scripting enhance productivity for advanced users?

Answer: The Terminal provides direct access to the Unix-based core of macOS. Shell scripting allows users to automate tasks, run commands, and create powerful workflows.

2. Provide examples of common shell commands used for productivity on macOS.

Answer: Examples include grep for searching, sed for text manipulation, awk for data extraction, and chmod for changing file permissions.

3. How can users create and execute shell scripts to automate tasks in macOS?

Answer: Users can create shell scripts using a text editor, save them with a .sh extension, make them executable using chmod +x, and run them from the Terminal.

Clipboard Management:

1. Explain the importance of clipboard management tools for productivity.

Answer: Clipboard managers enhance productivity by allowing users to store and retrieve multiple items from the clipboard history, eliminating the need to switch back and forth between applications.

2. What clipboard management tools are available for macOS, and how do they differ?

Answer: Tools like "Paste" and "Alfred" offer clipboard management features. They differ in terms of interface, search capabilities, and integration with other productivity tools.

3. How can users use clipboard managers to improve efficiency in tasks involving copy and paste?

Answer: Clipboard managers allow users to store a history of copied items, easily switch between them, and paste multiple items consecutively, streamlining repetitive copy-paste tasks.

Text Expander Tools:

1. What is the purpose of text expander tools, and how can they enhance typing efficiency?

Answer: Text expander tools allow users to create shortcuts for frequently used phrases or snippets, reducing the need to type repetitive text and improving typing speed.

2. Provide examples of scenarios where text expanders can significantly boost productivity.

Answer: Text expanders are useful for inserting email signatures, commonly used code snippets, addresses, and responses to frequently asked questions.

3. How can users create and manage text expansion snippets using dedicated tools?

Answer: Users can create and manage text expansion snippets in tools like "TextExpander" or "aText" by defining the shortcut and corresponding expanded text.

Task Management and To-Do Apps:

1. What features should users look for in a task management or to-do app for macOS?

Answer: Task management apps should offer features like due dates, reminders, priority levels, collaboration, and synchronization across devices.

2. How can users effectively use tags and labels in task management apps for organization?

Answer: Tags and labels allow users to categorize tasks by context, priority, or project, making it easier to filter and focus on specific groups of tasks.

3. Explain how task management apps can integrate with other productivity tools and services.

Answer: Many task management apps integrate with calendars, email clients, and collaboration tools, ensuring a seamless workflow and centralized access to tasks.

Calendar and Scheduling Tools:

1. How can users maximize productivity using calendar applications on macOS?

Answer: Calendar apps help users schedule and manage appointments, meetings, and events. Utilizing features like reminders and shared calendars enhances productivity.

2. Explain how calendar applications integrate with other productivity tools, such as email and task management.

Answer: Calendar apps often integrate with email clients, allowing users to create events directly from emails. Integration with task management apps ensures that scheduled tasks are reflected in the calendar.

3. Provide examples of advanced features in calendar applications that improve time management.

Answer: Advanced features may include the ability to set goals, track travel time, receive smart suggestions for meeting times, and integrate with location-based services.

File Management and Organization:

1. How can users effectively organize files and folders on macOS for enhanced productivity?

Answer: Creating a logical folder structure, using descriptive file names, and leveraging tags or color labels can improve file organization and retrieval.

2. What role do file syncing and cloud storage services play in file management productivity?

Answer: File syncing and cloud storage services like iCloud Drive or Dropbox enable users to access files from multiple devices, collaborate with others, and ensure data backup.

3. How can users utilize metadata and file attributes to streamline file searches on macOS?

Answer: Adding metadata such as comments, tags, or ratings to files enhances searchability. Users can use the Finder's search bar to filter files based on these attributes.

Password Managers:

1. Explain the significance of password managers for productivity and security.

Answer: Password managers store and generate complex passwords, reducing the cognitive load of remembering multiple passwords and enhancing overall online security.

2. How do password managers integrate with web browsers and applications on macOS?

Answer: Password managers often integrate as browser extensions, offering seamless autofill of login credentials. Some also integrate with macOS keychain for broader application support.

3. What security considerations should users keep in mind when selecting and using a password manager?

Answer: Users should choose a reputable password manager with strong encryption, enable multi-factor authentication, and regularly update passwords for optimal security.

Note-Taking and Documentation Apps:

1. What features should users look for in note-taking and documentation apps for macOS?

Answer: Features may include markdown support, organization with notebooks and tags, collaboration, integration with other apps, and accessibility across devices.

2. How can users effectively use templates and formatting options in note-taking apps?

Answer: Templates provide a structured starting point for notes, while formatting options allow users to create visually appealing and well-organized documentation.

3. Explain the role of document linking and cross-referencing in enhancing productivity in note-taking apps.

Answer: Document linking and cross-referencing allow users to connect related notes, making it easier to navigate and find information within a note-taking app.

Cloud Collaboration and Communication Tools:

1. How can cloud collaboration tools such as Google Workspace or Microsoft 365 enhance productivity on macOS?

Answer: Cloud collaboration tools enable real-time collaboration, file sharing, and communication among team members, fostering efficient teamwork.

2. Explain the integration of communication tools like Slack or Microsoft Teams with macOS productivity.

Answer: Communication tools integrate with macOS to provide instant messaging, file sharing, and video conferencing, promoting seamless collaboration and reducing the need for external communication apps.

3. What security measures should be considered when using cloud collaboration tools on macOS?

Answer: Users should enable two-factor authentication, carefully manage access permissions, and be aware of data encryption and privacy policies to ensure secure collaboration.

Mind Mapping and Visual Organization Tools:

1. How can mind mapping tools enhance creativity and organization in macOS?

Answer: Mind mapping tools allow users to visually organize ideas, concepts, and tasks. They stimulate creative thinking and provide a structured representation of interconnected information.

2. What are some popular mind mapping applications for macOS, and how do they differ?

Answer: Applications like MindNode, XMind, and iThoughtsX offer diverse features for mind mapping, including collaboration, export options, and integration with other productivity tools.

3. Provide examples of scenarios where mind mapping can be particularly beneficial for productivity.

Answer: Mind mapping is useful for brainstorming sessions, project planning, outlining complex topics, and organizing thoughts before writing or presenting.

Virtual Desktops and Window Management:

1. How can users benefit from virtual desktops and window management tools in macOS?

Answer: Virtual desktops allow users to organize and switch between different workspaces, while window management tools streamline the arrangement and resizing of open application windows.

2. Explain how Mission Control and Spaces contribute to effective multitasking on macOS.

Answer: Mission Control provides an overview of open windows and virtual desktops, while Spaces allows users to create multiple desktops for organizing different tasks or projects.

3. How can users customize and optimize window management settings for their workflow?

Answer: Users can customize window management settings in "System Preferences" > "Mission Control," adjusting options such as hot corners, gestures, and display arrangement.

Backup and Disaster Recovery Tools:

1. What strategies and tools can users employ for effective backup and disaster recovery on macOS?

Answer: Time Machine is a built-in backup tool, and users can also leverage third-party solutions like Carbon Copy Cloner or SuperDuper for additional features and customization.

App Store and Software Installation

App Store Usage:

1. How does the App Store on macOS contribute to the user experience?

Answer: The App Store provides a centralized platform for discovering, purchasing, and installing applications, making it convenient for users to find and manage software.

2. What types of applications are typically available on the App Store, and how are they categorized?

Answer: The App Store offers a wide range of applications, including productivity tools, games, utilities, and more. They are categorized for easy navigation, such as Productivity, Utilities, Games, and so on.

3. How can users check for updates and manage installed applications from the App Store?

Answer: Users can check for updates in the "Updates" tab of the App Store. Installed applications can be managed in the "Purchased" tab, allowing users to reinstall or update apps.

Software Updates and Upgrades:

1. Explain the importance of keeping software up to date on macOS.

Answer: Keeping software updated is crucial for security, bug fixes, and accessing new features. It ensures that the system is running efficiently and is protected against vulnerabilities.

2. How can users configure software update settings on macOS for automatic updates?

Answer: Users can configure automatic updates in "System Preferences" > "Software Update" by enabling the "Automatically keep my Mac up to date" option.

3. What considerations should users keep in mind before performing a major macOS system upgrade?

Answer: Before upgrading, users should check application compatibility, perform a backup using Time Machine, and ensure sufficient disk space for the upgrade.

Installing and Removing Applications:

1. Describe the process of installing an application from the App Store on macOS.

Answer: Users can open the App Store, browse or search for the desired app, click "Get" or the price button, and enter their Apple ID password to initiate the download and installation.

2. How can users install applications from third-party sources, and what precautions should be taken?

Answer: Users can install third-party apps by downloading them from the internet. Precautions include verifying the source, checking reviews, and ensuring the app is compatible with the macOS version.

3. What steps should users follow to uninstall an application on macOS?

Answer: Users can uninstall an app by dragging it from the "Applications" folder to the Trash. Some apps may have uninstallers provided by the developer for a complete removal.

App Permissions and Security:

1. How does macOS ensure the security of applications during installation?

Answer: macOS uses Gatekeeper to verify the identity of app developers and ensure apps haven't been tampered with. Apps from unidentified developers may require explicit permission to install.

2. What is the purpose of the "Privacy" settings in macOS, and how do they relate to app permissions?

Answer: Privacy settings allow users to control app access to sensitive data like contacts, calendars, and location. Users can manage these settings in "Security & Privacy" under the "Privacy" tab.

3. How can users troubleshoot issues related to app installations and permissions?

Answer: Users can check the system logs using the Console app for error messages, review app-specific settings in "Security & Privacy," and ensure the app is compatible with the macOS version.

Uninstalling and Troubleshooting Applications:

1. What steps should users take if they encounter issues with an application after installation?

Answer: Users can try reinstalling the app, checking for updates, reviewing the developer's support resources, or contacting the developer's customer support for assistance.

2. How can users troubleshoot common issues related to app installations and removals?

Answer: Troubleshooting may involve checking system logs for error messages, ensuring the app is compatible with the macOS version, and using uninstallers provided by developers for complete removal.

3. Explain the role of the "Applications" folder in macOS and its significance for app management.

Answer: The "Applications" folder is the default location for installing apps. It provides a centralized location for users to organize, locate, and manage their installed applications.

Gatekeeper and App Verification:

1. What is Gatekeeper, and how does it contribute to app security on macOS?

Answer: Gatekeeper is a security feature that ensures apps come from identified developers and haven't been altered. It helps protect users from downloading and running malicious software.

2. Can users adjust Gatekeeper settings to allow apps from different sources?

Answer: Yes, users can adjust Gatekeeper settings in "Security & Privacy" under "General" to allow apps from the App Store, identified developers, or from anywhere (with caution).

3. How does Gatekeeper handle the first launch of a newly downloaded app?

Answer: Gatekeeper checks the app's signature and notifies the user if the app is from an unidentified developer. Users can grant permission for the first launch in "Security & Privacy."

App Store Guidelines and Compliance:

1. Explain the guidelines that developers must follow to publish apps on the App Store.

Answer: Developers must adhere to Apple's App Store Review Guidelines, covering aspects like functionality, design, content, privacy, and ensuring compliance with Apple's policies.

2. How does Apple ensure the security and integrity of apps available on the App Store?

Answer: Apple reviews each app before it is published to the App Store, checking for security vulnerabilities, compliance with guidelines, and ensuring that the app meets quality standards.

3. What steps should developers take to ensure their apps comply with App Store guidelines?

Answer: Developers should thoroughly review the App Store Review Guidelines, test their apps for quality and security, and address any issues raised during the review process.

macOS Software Packaging and Distribution:

1. How are macOS apps typically packaged and distributed for installation?

Answer:macOS apps are often packaged as ".dmg" (Disk Image) files or ".pkg" (Package) files. Users download these files, open them, and follow on-screen instructions to install the app.

2. Explain the difference between installing apps from the App Store and installing apps from other sources.

Answer: Installing from the App Store is streamlined, and apps are vetted by Apple. Installing from other sources may require manual download, verification, and careful attention to security.

3. What is the purpose of code signing in macOS software distribution, and how does it benefit users?

Answer: Code signing ensures the integrity of the app by adding a digital signature. It benefits users by verifying that the app hasn't been altered since it was signed by the developer.

System Integrity Protection (SIP):

1. What is System Integrity Protection (SIP), and how does it impact the installation and modification of applications?

Answer:SIP protects critical system files and directories from modification, including those related to installed applications. It prevents unauthorized changes to the system.

2. Can users disable SIP, and under what circumstances might they consider doing so?

Answer: While it is possible to disable SIP, it is generally not recommended for security reasons. Disabling SIP may be necessary for specific system modifications, but caution is advised.

3. How can users check the SIP status on their macOS system?

Answer: Users can check SIP status by opening the Terminal and running the command csrutil status. The output indicates whether SIP is enabled or disabled.

Mac App Notarization:

1. What is app notarization, and how does it contribute to the security of macOS applications?

Answer: App notarization is a process where Apple checks and confirms that an app is free of malicious content. Notarized apps are more likely to pass through Gatekeeper.

2. How can developers notarize their applications before distribution?

Answer: Developers can notarize their apps using Xcode or the altool command-line tool. Notarization involves submitting the app to Apple for review and approval.

3. What are the benefits for users when installing notarized applications on macOS?

Answer: Notarized apps have been scanned for security threats, providing users with an additional layer of assurance that the app is from a reputable source and free from malware.

Command-Line Installation Tools:

1. Can you explain the use of package managers like Homebrew for installing software on macOS?

Answer: Homebrew is a package manager for macOS that simplifies the installation of command-line tools and software. Users can install, update, and remove packages with a few simple commands.

2. What are the advantages and potential risks of using command-line installation tools for software?

Answer: Advantages include ease of installation and version management. Risks may include dependency conflicts and potential security concerns if not used carefully.

3. How can users troubleshoot issues related to command-line installations, such as dependency conflicts?

Answer: Users can check error messages in the Terminal, review documentation for the specific package, and seek assistance from online forums or the package's community.

App Store Business Model and Purchases:

1. How does the App Store business model work, and how do developers monetize their apps?

Answer: Developers can monetize apps through various models, including one-time purchases, subscriptions, and in-app purchases. Apple takes a percentage of revenue from paid apps and in-app purchases.

2. What considerations should developers keep in mind when setting the pricing model for their apps on the App Store?

Answer: Developers should consider factors like the app's value, target audience, competition, and the perceived willingness of users to pay for the app or related services.

3. How can users manage and review their App Store purchases on macOS?

Answer: Users can view their App Store purchases in the "Purchased" tab of the App Store. This includes a history of apps they have downloaded or purchased.

Family Sharing and App Bundles:

1. Explain the concept of Family Sharing on the App Store and how it benefits users.

Answer: Family Sharing allows users to share purchases, subscriptions, and certain iCloud services with their family members. It promotes cost-sharing and centralized management.

2. What are app bundles on the App Store, and how do they benefit both developers and users?

Answer: App bundles allow developers to package multiple apps together at a discounted price. Users benefit from cost savings compared to purchasing individual apps.

3. Can users gift apps to others on the App Store, and how does the gifting process work?

Answer: Yes, users can gift apps to others on the App Store. They can choose the app, click the "Share" button, and select the "Gift App" option, entering the recipient's email address.

App Store Review Process:

1. Can you outline the App Store review process, and what are some common reasons for apps to be rejected?

Answer: The App Store review process involves checks for functionality, design, content, and adherence to guidelines. Common reasons for rejection include bugs, incomplete information, and violations of guidelines.

mac OS Package Management

Homebrew:

1. What is Homebrew, and how does it simplify package management on macOS?

Answer: Homebrew is a package manager for macOS that simplifies the installation of software and command-line tools. It automates the process of downloading, compiling, and installing packages.

2. How can you install a package using Homebrew, and what are the advantages of using it?

Answer: You can install a package with brew install [package]. Homebrew simplifies dependency management, ensures packages are up to date, and provides an organized structure for installed software.

3. Explain the process of updating all installed packages with Homebrew.

Answer: Use the command brew update to update Homebrew itself, followed by brew upgrade to update all installed packages to their latest versions.

MacPorts:

1. What is MacPorts, and how does it differ from Homebrew?

Answer: MacPorts is another package manager for macOS. It focuses on providing a more traditional UNIX-like experience and often involves compiling packages from source.

2. How can you install a package using MacPorts, and what considerations should be kept in mind?

Answer: Use the command sudo port install [package] to install a package. It's important to note that MacPorts requires administrative privileges for installations.

3. Compare the advantages and disadvantages of using MacPorts over Homebrew.

Answer: MacPorts allows for more fine-grained control and customization but may involve longer compilation times. Homebrew offers a simpler user experience with precompiled binaries.

Fink:

1. What is Fink, and how does it contribute to package management on macOS?

Answer: Fink is a package manager for macOS that brings Unix/Linux software to macOS. It provides a wide range of precompiled packages that can be easily installed.

2. How can you install a package using Fink, and what types of software does it typically manage?

Answer: Use the command fink install [package] to install a package. Fink manages a variety of software, including command-line tools, libraries, and graphical applications.

3. Discuss the role of Fink in maintaining a UNIX-like environment on macOS.

Answer: Fink plays a crucial role in providing a UNIX-like environment on macOS by offering a repository of software commonly found on UNIX/Linux systems.

Package Building and Compilation:

1. Explain the concept of package building in the context of macOS package management.

Answer: Package building involves compiling source code to create executable binaries suitable for the macOS environment. It ensures compatibility and optimization for the target system.

2. What challenges might arise during the compilation process, and how can they be addressed?

Answer: Challenges may include missing dependencies or compatibility issues. They can be addressed by installing required libraries, adjusting compilation flags, or seeking community support.

3. How can users troubleshoot issues related to failed package builds or installations?

Answer: Users can check error messages during the compilation process, review documentation for the specific package, and seek assistance from community forums or the package's developers.

Package Dependency Management:

1. Why is managing dependencies crucial in package management, and how do package managers handle this task?

Answer: Managing dependencies ensures that a software package has all the necessary components to run. Package managers like Homebrew, MacPorts, and Fink automatically handle dependency resolution.

2. How can users view and manage dependencies for a specific package using package management tools?

Answer: Users can view dependencies with commands like brew info [package] (Homebrew), port deps [package] (MacPorts), or fink list -i [package] (Fink). Dependency management is handled automatically during installations.

3. Discuss strategies for resolving conflicts or compatibility issues between package dependencies.

Answer: Strategies may include adjusting versions of conflicting dependencies, using virtual environments, or consulting the community for guidance on resolving specific issues.

Package Versioning and Rollbacks:

1. Why is versioning important in package management, and how do package managers handle multiple versions of the same software?

Answer: Versioning ensures that users can install specific versions of software. Package managers maintain a version history, and users can switch between versions if needed.

2. How can users install a specific version of a package using Homebrew, MacPorts, or Fink?

Answer: For Homebrew, users can use brew install [package]@version. For MacPorts, it's sudo port install [package]@[version]. Fink provides similar version-specific installation commands.

3. Discuss the importance of rollbacks in package management and how users can perform them.

Answer: Rollbacks allow users to revert to a previous state if an update causes issues. Some package managers support rollbacks through commands like brew switch, port activate, or fink selfupdate.

Package Repositories and Sources:

1. What is the role of package repositories in macOS package management?

Answer: Package repositories are central collections of software packages. Package managers use these repositories to download, install, and update software on macOS.

2. How can users add, remove, or manage package repositories in Homebrew, MacPorts, or Fink?

Answer: For Homebrew, users can use brew tap to add or remove repositories. MacPorts and Fink typically involve modifying configuration files or using specific commands to manage repositories.

3. What considerations should users keep in mind when adding third-party repositories to their package manager?

Answer: Users should ensure that third-party repositories are reputable, well-maintained, and compatible with their macOS version to avoid potential security or compatibility issues.

Integration with System Libraries:

1. Explain how package managers on macOS integrate with system libraries and frameworks.

Answer: Package managers ensure that installed packages use or link against system libraries and frameworks. They maintain compatibility and prevent conflicts with existing system components.

2. What challenges might arise when packages require specific versions of system libraries, and how can users address them?

Answer: Challenges may include conflicts with existing system libraries. Users can use package manager options to link against specific versions or adjust the library path to avoid conflicts.

3. How do package managers contribute to maintaining a clean and organized system environment on macOS?

Answer: Package managers install software in designated directories and manage dependencies, ensuring a clean and organized environment. They provide tools to uninstall, upgrade, or remove software cleanly.

Community Support and Documentation:

1. How can users leverage community support when encountering issues with package management on macOS?

Answer: Users can participate in forums, mailing lists, or online communities specific to the package manager they are using. Seeking help from experienced users or developers can provide valuable insights.

2. Discuss the importance of documentation in the context of macOS package management.

Answer: Documentation provides users with guidance on installation, usage, troubleshooting, and best practices. Package managers often have detailed documentation to help users navigate the system.

3. How can users contribute to the improvement of package management tools or share their experiences with the community?

Answer: Users can contribute by reporting issues, submitting bug fixes, or participating in discussions on forums and mailing lists. Sharing experiences helps others navigate potential challenges.

Package Management Best Practices:

1. What are some best practices for managing packages on macOS to ensure a stable and efficient system?

Answer: Best practices include regularly updating packages, using version-specific installations when necessary, managing dependencies carefully, and staying informed about changes in package manager behavior.

2. How can users ensure that packages are securely downloaded and installed on macOS?

Answer: Users should only download packages from reputable sources and verify checksums when provided. Package managers like Homebrew, MacPorts, and Fink have built-in security features.

3. Discuss the role of sandboxing and isolation in package management on macOS.

Answer: Package managers often install software in isolated environments or directories, minimizing the impact on the overall system. This helps prevent conflicts and ensures a clean installation.

System Security and Package Trustworthiness:

1. How do package managers on macOS contribute to system security?

Answer: Package managers verify the authenticity and integrity of packages, ensuring they come from trusted sources. They also provide mechanisms for users to verify downloads.

2. What precautions should users take to maintain a secure package management environment on macOS?

Answer: Users should regularly update packages, avoid using untrusted repositories, and review permissions before granting administrative access during installations.

3. Can users customize security settings within package managers to enhance the protection of their system?

Answer: Yes, users can configure security settings within package managers, such as adjusting repository sources, verifying downloads, and using HTTPS for communication.

Enterprise Deployment and Configuration Management:

1. How can package managers be utilized for enterprise deployment and configuration management on macOS?

Answer: Package managers can automate the deployment of software across multiple machines, ensuring consistency in the software environment for enterprise users.

2. Discuss strategies for managing configurations and settings when deploying packages to multiple systems.

Answer: Some package managers provide options for configuring settings during installation. For more complex configurations, users may leverage additional tools or scripts for customization.

3. What challenges might arise when deploying packages in an enterprise environment, and how can they be addressed?

Answer: Challenges may include network limitations or the need for specific configurations. Addressing these challenges may involve working closely with IT teams, testing deployments, and ensuring compatibility.

Package Manager Extensibility and Plugins:

1. Can users extend the functionality of package managers on macOS through plugins or extensions?

Answer: Some package managers, like Homebrew, support extensions or plugins to add additional functionality or integrate with other tools. Users can explore available plugins based on their needs.

2. Provide examples of scenarios where users might benefit from customizing or extending their package manager's functionality.

Answer: Examples include creating custom taps in Homebrew for niche software, developing plugins for specific use cases, or integrating package management with other automation tools.

3. How can users discover and install plugins or extensions for their preferred package manager?

Answer: Users can typically find documentation or community resources for extensions. For example, Homebrew users can explore the available taps or plugins on GitHub.

Future Trends in macOS Package Management:

1. What are some emerging trends or developments in macOS package management, and how might they shape the future?

Answer: Emerging trends include the use of containerization, improved security measures, and efforts to streamline cross-platform compatibility. Continuous improvement in user experience and security is likely to be a focus.

ONLINE RESOURCES

Practice PaperLink:https://forms.gle/3tjAjxTYdXFv7EHX8

QR Code:

Video Link:https://www.youtube.com/playlist?list=PLzlh_31VWEFpGBHf2btDfkIXVAf7ndV4c

QR Code:

Chapter 8: mac OS Networking

Network Setup and Configuration

Network Basics:

1. Explain the process of setting up a wired network connection on macOS.

Answer: Navigate to "System Preferences" > "Network," select the desired interface (e.g., Ethernet), click "Advanced," and configure settings such as IP address and DNS.

2. How can a user troubleshoot common issues with network connectivity on macOS?

Answer: Check hardware connections, verify network settings, use the Network Diagnostics tool, reset the network configuration, and update network drivers if needed.

3. Describe the steps to configure a static IP address on a macOS device.

Answer: In "System Preferences" > "Network," choose the network interface, click "Advanced," and select "Manually" under "Configure IPv4." Enter the desired IP address, subnet mask, and DNS.

Wireless Networking:

1. How does macOS handle the setup of Wi-Fi networks, and what considerations should users be aware of?

Answer: Users can connect to Wi-Fi networks in "System Preferences" > "Network." Considerations include network security (WPA/WPA2), signal strength, and potential interference.

2. Explain the process of prioritizing Wi-Fi networks on macOS.

Answer: In "System Preferences" > "Network," click "Wi-Fi," then "Advanced." Drag preferred networks to the top of the list to prioritize them.

3. What security measures should users implement when setting up a Wi-Fi network on macOS?

Answer: Use strong encryption (WPA3 if available), enable network password protection, and consider hiding the network SSID to enhance security.

Network Protocols:

1. What is the role of the DNS (Domain Name System) in network configuration, and how can users configure DNS settings on macOS?

Answer:DNS resolves domain names to IP addresses. Users can configure DNS in "System Preferences" > "Network" by selecting the network interface, clicking "Advanced," and choosing the "DNS" tab.

2. Explain the purpose of DHCP (Dynamic Host Configuration Protocol) in network setups.

Answer:DHCP dynamically assigns IP addresses to devices on a network. It simplifies network administration by automating the IP configuration process.

3. How can a user configure a macOS device to use a specific DNS server instead of obtaining it automatically?

Answer: In "System Preferences" > "Network," select the network interface, click "Advanced," and go to the "DNS" tab. Add the desired DNS server addresses manually.

Network Sharing and Personal Hotspot:

1. Describe the steps to set up and configure Internet Sharing on macOS.

Answer: In "System Preferences" > "Sharing," select "Internet Sharing," choose the internet source (e.g., Ethernet), and specify the shared connection (e.g., Wi-Fi).

2. How can a macOS device be used as a Personal Hotspot to share its cellular data connection?

Answer: In "Settings" > "Personal Hotspot" on iOS, enable the feature, set a Wi-Fi password, and connect the macOS device to the hotspot in "System Preferences" > "Network."

3. What security considerations should users keep in mind when sharing their internet connection on macOS?

Answer: Use a strong Wi-Fi password, consider enabling WPA3 if supported, and monitor connected devices to ensure only authorized users are accessing the shared network.

Advanced Network Configuration:

1. Explain the purpose of the "Locations" feature in macOS network settings.

Answer:"Locations" allow users to save and switch between different network configurations. This is useful for adapting to various network environments.

2. How can users configure a macOS device to use a proxy server for internet access?

Answer: In "System Preferences" > "Network," select the network interface, click "Advanced," and go to the "Proxies" tab. Configure the proxy settings as needed.

3. Discuss the use of VLANs (Virtual LANs) and how they can be configured on macOS.

Answer:VLANs are used to logically segment a network. On macOS, VLANs can be configured in "System Preferences" > "Network" by adding a virtual interface for each VLAN.

Network Troubleshooting:

1. What steps can users take to troubleshoot a macOS device that is unable to connect to the internet?

Answer: Check network cables and Wi-Fi signal, verify IP configuration, use Network Diagnostics, restart the router, and ensure no firewall is blocking internet access.

2. How can users troubleshoot DNS-related issues on macOS?

Answer: Verify DNS server settings, try using a different DNS server, flush DNS cache using the Terminal command sudo dscacheutil -flushcache, and check for software or hardware firewall issues.

3. What role does the Network Utility tool play in diagnosing network issues on macOS?

Answer: Network Utility provides tools like Ping, Traceroute, and Netstat to diagnose network problems. Users can access it in "Applications" > "Utilities."

VPN (Virtual Private Network):

1. Explain the purpose of a VPN, and how can users set up and configure a VPN connection on macOS?

Answer:A VPN provides a secure connection over the internet. In "System Preferences" > "Network," users can add a VPN connection by selecting the "+" button.

2. What security considerations should users be aware of when using a VPN on macOS?

Answer: Ensure the VPN uses strong encryption (e.g., OpenVPN or IKEv2), regularly update VPN software, and only use reputable VPN services.

3. Discuss common issues users may encounter when configuring or using a VPN on macOS.

Answer: Issues may include connection drops, authentication problems, or conflicts with other network configurations. Troubleshooting may involve checking settings, logs, and consulting the VPN service provider.

Network Security:

1. How can users enhance the security of their home network on macOS?

Answer: Enable WPA3 for Wi-Fi security, use a strong router password, regularly update router firmware, and consider implementing MAC address filtering for additional security.

2. Explain the purpose of a firewall on macOS, and how can users configure firewall settings?

Answer: The firewall on macOS controls incoming and outgoing network traffic. Users can configure it in "System Preferences" > "Security & Privacy" > "Firewall."

3. What is the role of the "Stealth Mode" in macOS firewall settings, and when might it be useful?

Answer: Stealth Mode prevents the computer from responding to unsolicited network traffic. It can be useful for additional security by not revealing the presence of the computer to potential attackers.

Command-Line Network Tools:

1. How can users use the Terminal and command-line tools to gather information about network connections on macOS?

Answer: Commands like netstat, ifconfig, and ping can provide details about network interfaces, connections, and test network reachability.

2. Explain the purpose of the traceroute command, and how can it be used for network troubleshooting?

Answer:traceroute traces the route that packets take to reach a destination. It helps identify network bottlenecks or connectivity issues between the source and destination.

3. What is the significance of the nslookup command, and how does it differ from other DNS-related commands?

Answer:nslookup is used to query DNS servers for domain information. It differs from other DNS commands by providing more detailed information about DNS records.

Network Monitoring and Logging:

1. How can users monitor network activity on macOS, and what tools are available for this purpose?

Answer: Tools like Little Snitch or built-in utilities like Activity Monitor and Console can be used to monitor network activity and log network-related events.

2. Discuss the importance of log files in diagnosing and troubleshooting network issues on macOS.

Answer: Log files provide valuable information about network-related events. Users can review logs in the Console app to identify issues and trends.

3. How can users configure macOS to log specific network events or activities?

Answer: Users can configure logging preferences in "System Preferences" > "Security & Privacy" > "Advanced" to specify the types of events to be logged.

Network Time Configuration:

1. Why is accurate time synchronization important for networked systems, and how does macOS handle time synchronization?

Answer: Accurate time synchronization is crucial for coordination and security. macOS uses the Network Time Protocol (NTP) to synchronize time with remote servers.

2. How can users configure time settings, including time zone and NTP servers, on macOS?

Answer: In "System Preferences" > "Date & Time," users can set the time zone and configure NTP servers by clicking "Time Zone" or "Date & Time" > "Open Date & Time Preferences."

Bonjour and Zero Configuration Networking:

1. Explain the purpose of Bonjour and how it facilitates zero-configuration networking on macOS.

Answer: Bonjour is Apple's implementation of zero-configuration networking, allowing devices to discover and communicate with each other without manual configuration.

2. What types of services and applications benefit from Bonjour on macOS?

Answer: Bonjour is commonly used for file sharing, printer discovery, and multiplayer gaming. It simplifies the setup of network services in a local environment.

Network File Sharing:

1. How can users enable and configure file sharing on macOS, allowing other devices to access shared folders?

Answer: In "System Preferences" > "Sharing," users can enable "File Sharing" and configure shared folders. Permissions can be set to control access.

2. Discuss the security considerations users should keep in mind when enabling file sharing on macOS.

Answer: Use strong passwords for shared folders, limit access to specific users or groups, and consider using encrypted protocols like SMB or AFP for file sharing.

Network Backup and Time Machine:

1. How does Time Machine utilize the network for backups, and how can users configure Time Machine to back up to a network location?

Answer: Time Machine can back up to a network-attached storage (NAS) device. Users can select the network location in "System Preferences" > "Time Machine."

2. What challenges might users face when performing network backups using Time Machine, and how can they address these challenges?

Answer: Challenges may include network interruptions or slow performance. Users can address these issues by ensuring a stable network connection and optimizing network settings.

IPv6 Configuration:

1. Why is IPv6 important, and how does macOS handle IPv6 configuration?

Answer:IPv6 provides a larger address space than IPv4. macOS supports IPv6, and devices can automatically configure IPv6 addresses if the network supports it.

2. How can users verify and troubleshoot IPv6 connectivity on macOS?

Answer: Users can use the ifconfig command to view IPv6 addresses, use ping6 to test connectivity, and check network settings in "System Preferences" > "Network."

Wi-Fi and Bluetooth Settings

Wi-Fi Settings:

1. How can users access and configure Wi-Fi settings on macOS?

Answer: Wi-Fi settings can be accessed in "System Preferences" > "Network." Users can select the Wi-Fi interface and configure connection details.

2. Explain the process of connecting to a Wi-Fi network on macOS.

Answer: Click the Wi-Fi icon in the menu bar, select the desired network, enter the password if required, and click "Join."

3. What factors should be considered when troubleshooting Wi-Fi connectivity issues on macOS?

Answer: Check signal strength, verify network credentials, restart the router, update Wi-Fi drivers, and use the Wireless Diagnostics tool for more in-depth troubleshooting.

Advanced Wi-Fi Settings:

1. Describe the steps to prioritize Wi-Fi networks on macOS.

Answer: In "System Preferences" > "Network," click "Wi-Fi," then "Advanced." Drag preferred networks to the top of the list.

2. How can users forget a Wi-Fi network on macOS, and when might this be necessary?

Answer: In "System Preferences" > "Network," select Wi-Fi, click "Advanced," choose the network, and click "Forget." This might be necessary for troubleshooting or security reasons.

3. Explain the significance of the "Location" feature in macOS Wi-Fi settings.

Answer:"Locations" allow users to save and switch between different Wi-Fi configurations, useful for adapting to various network environments.

Wi-Fi Security:

1. What security measures should users implement when connecting to a Wi-Fi network on macOS?

Answer: Use WPA3 if available, enable password protection, and avoid connecting to open, unsecured networks.

2. Discuss the importance of MAC address filtering for Wi-Fi security.

Answer:MAC address filtering allows users to specify which devices can connect to the Wi-Fi network, enhancing security by limiting access.

3. How can users view information about their current Wi-Fi connection, including signal strength and network details?

Answer: Option-click the Wi-Fi icon in the menu bar to reveal detailed information about the current connection.

Bluetooth Settings:

1. Where can users access and configure Bluetooth settings on macOS?

Answer: Bluetooth settings are in "System Preferences" > "Bluetooth." Users can turn Bluetooth on or off, manage connected devices, and configure preferences.

2. Explain the process of pairing a Bluetooth device with macOS.

Answer: In "System Preferences" > "Bluetooth," ensure Bluetooth is on, select "Open Bluetooth Preferences," and follow the instructions for pairing the specific device.

3. How can users troubleshoot common Bluetooth connectivity issues on macOS?

Answer: Ensure Bluetooth is enabled, restart Bluetooth, update macOS and device firmware, and remove and re-pair devices if needed.

Advanced Bluetooth Settings:

1. Describe the steps to remove a paired Bluetooth device from macOS.

Answer: In "System Preferences" > "Bluetooth," select the device and click the "X" next to it to remove the pairing.

2. What is the significance of the "Allow Handoff between this Mac and your iCloud devices" option in Bluetooth settings?

Answer: Enabling this option allows users to seamlessly switch tasks between their Mac and other iCloud-connected devices.

3. How can users customize the name and icon associated with their Mac's Bluetooth identity?

Answer: In "System Preferences" > "Sharing," users can change the computer name, affecting Bluetooth identity.

Bluetooth Security:

1. Why is it important for users to be cautious about Bluetooth security on macOS?

Answer: Bluetooth connections can be susceptible to unauthorized access or interference. Users should enable secure pairing and keep Bluetooth up to date.

2. Discuss the security considerations when using Bluetooth devices with macOS, such as wireless keyboards or headphones.

Answer: Users should ensure devices use secure Bluetooth connections (e.g., Bluetooth 4.2 or newer), regularly update device firmware, and avoid using unsecured connections.

3. How can users protect their macOS device from potential Bluetooth attacks or vulnerabilities?

Answer: Keep macOS and Bluetooth firmware up to date, disable Bluetooth when not in use, and be cautious about pairing with unknown devices.

Continuity Features:

1. What are Continuity features in macOS, and how do they leverage Wi-Fi and Bluetooth?

Answer: Continuity features, such as Handoff and Universal Clipboard, use Wi-Fi and Bluetooth to seamlessly transfer tasks between Apple devices.

2. How can users enable and use Handoff between their macOS device and other Apple devices?

Answer: Ensure Bluetooth is on, and Handoff is enabled in "System Preferences" > "General." Compatible tasks can then be transferred between devices.

3. Discuss the role of Wi-Fi and Bluetooth in enabling AirDrop functionality on macOS.

Answer: AirDrop uses both Wi-Fi and Bluetooth for device discovery and file transfer. Devices need to be within Bluetooth range for successful AirDrop.

Troubleshooting Wi-Fi and Bluetooth Interference:

1. How can users identify and resolve interference issues between Wi-Fi and Bluetooth on macOS?

Answer: Use different Wi-Fi channels, relocate Wi-Fi router or Bluetooth devices, and update firmware to mitigate interference.

2. What steps can users take to troubleshoot Bluetooth interference with other wireless devices?

Answer: Keep devices within Bluetooth range, avoid placing devices near potential sources of interference, and update Bluetooth drivers if available.

3. Discuss the role of signal strength and range in troubleshooting Wi-Fi and Bluetooth connectivity issues.

Answer: Weak signal strength or being out of range can cause connectivity problems. Users should optimize the placement of routers and devices for better coverage.

Wi-Fi and Bluetooth Logs:

1. How can users access and interpret logs related to Wi-Fi and Bluetooth on macOS for troubleshooting?

Answer: Users can view system logs in the Console app for information on Wi-Fi and Bluetooth events. These logs can help diagnose connectivity issues.

2. Discuss the types of information available in macOS logs related to Wi-Fi and Bluetooth.

Answer: Logs may include information on connection attempts, signal strength, device discovery, and error messages related to Wi-Fi and Bluetooth events.

Wi-Fi and Bluetooth Performance Optimization:

1. How can users optimize Wi-Fi performance on macOS for better speed and reliability?

Answer: Choose optimal Wi-Fi channels, update router firmware, use a dual-band router, and minimize interference from other devices.

2. What strategies can users employ to enhance Bluetooth performance and reduce latency on macOS?

Answer: Keep devices within close proximity, update Bluetooth firmware, avoid interference from other electronic devices, and use Bluetooth 4.2 or newer for improved performance.

Location-Based Services and Privacy:

1. Explain how macOS uses Wi-Fi and Bluetooth for location-based services, such as geolocation.

Answer:macOS uses Wi-Fi and Bluetooth to determine the device's location based on nearby Wi-Fi networks and Bluetooth devices.

2. How can users manage location-based services and privacy settings related to Wi-Fi and Bluetooth on macOS?

Answer: In "System Preferences" > "Security & Privacy" > "Location Services," users can manage permissions for individual apps and system services.

Wi-Fi and Bluetooth Energy Efficiency:

1. Discuss the energy-efficient features in macOS related to Wi-Fi and Bluetooth.

Answer:macOS uses technologies like Wake on Demand and Power Nap to minimize power consumption while maintaining connectivity.

2. How can users configure macOS to optimize energy efficiency for Wi-Fi and Bluetooth?

Answer: In "System Preferences" > "Energy Saver," users can adjust settings to optimize energy efficiency. Disabling Wi-Fi or Bluetooth when not in use also conserves power.

Wireless Diagnostics Tool:

1. Explain the purpose of the Wireless Diagnostics tool on macOS, and how can users utilize it for troubleshooting?

Answer: Wireless Diagnostics provides detailed information about Wi-Fi networks and can assist in diagnosing connectivity issues. It can be accessed by Option-clicking the Wi-Fi icon.

2. What specific features and tools are available within the Wireless Diagnostics tool for Wi-Fi troubleshooting?

Answer: Wireless Diagnostics includes features such as Scan, Performance, and Sniffer, allowing users to analyze Wi-Fi networks, monitor performance, and capture packets for in-depth troubleshooting.

Integration with Other Apple Devices:

1. How do Wi-Fi and Bluetooth settings on macOS integrate with other Apple devices, such as iPhones and iPads?

Answer: Wi-Fi and Bluetooth settings facilitate features like Handoff, AirDrop, and device continuity, enabling seamless integration and collaboration across Apple devices.

2. What considerations should users keep in mind when using Wi-Fi and Bluetooth settings to connect macOS devices with other Apple devices?

Answer: Ensure devices are signed in with the same Apple ID, use up-to-date operating systems, and enable Handoff and other continuity features for a seamless experience.

Future Trends in Wi-Fi and Bluetooth Technology:

1. What are some emerging trends or developments in Wi-Fi and Bluetooth technology, and how might they shape the future of connectivity on macOS?

Answer: Trends include Wi-Fi 6 and Bluetooth 5 advancements, increased integration with IoT devices, and enhanced security features. Future macOS updates are likely to adopt these technologies for improved connectivity.

2. How might the evolution of Wi-Fi and Bluetooth standards impact the user experience on macOS devices in the coming years?

Answer: New standards will likely bring faster speeds, improved range, and better energy efficiency. Users can expect enhanced performance and connectivity with evolving Wi-Fi and Bluetooth technologies.

3. Discuss potential challenges and solutions related to the integration of Wi-Fi and Bluetooth with emerging technologies, such as 5G and edge computing.

Answer: Challenges may include ensuring compatibility and optimizing coexistence. Solutions involve collaborative efforts among technology providers to create seamless integration protocols.

4. In what ways might Wi-Fi and Bluetooth technologies on macOS contribute to the overall ecosystem of smart homes and connected devices?

Answer: Wi-Fi and Bluetooth play key roles in connecting and controlling smart home devices. As macOS integrates with this ecosystem, users can expect a more unified and interconnected experience.

Troubleshooting Network Issues

General Network Troubleshooting:

1. What steps do you take when a macOS device is unable to connect to the internet?

Answer:I would first check the network cables, Wi-Fi signal strength, and ensure the correct network settings. Then, I might use Network Diagnostics or check for potential router issues.

2. How do you troubleshoot slow internet speeds on a macOS device?

Answer:I would check the network bandwidth, run speed tests, and analyze network utilization using tools like Activity Monitor. If needed, I might optimize Wi-Fi channels or investigate potential interference.

3. Describe your approach to troubleshooting intermittent Wi-Fi connectivity issues on macOS.

Answer:I would check for signal interference, update Wi-Fi drivers, review system logs for connection drops, and consider adjusting router settings. If necessary, I might change the Wi-Fi channel.

Wired Network Troubleshooting:

1. What steps would you take to troubleshoot a macOS device with no wired network connection?

Answer:I would check the Ethernet cable, verify that the network interface is active, and use Network Diagnostics to identify and resolve issues. Additionally, I might review system logs for relevant information.

2. How do you diagnose and resolve issues with a macOS device that cannot obtain an IP address via DHCP?

Answer:I would check the DHCP server, verify network settings, and use the Terminal to release and renew the IP address. If needed, I might manually configure a static IP for troubleshooting.

3. Discuss the steps you would take to troubleshoot packet loss on a wired network connection in macOS.

Answer:I would use tools like Ping or traceroute to identify packet loss, inspect network cables, check for interference, and review network configurations. If necessary, I might replace faulty hardware.

Wireless Network Troubleshooting:

1. How do you troubleshoot a macOS device that cannot detect any Wi-Fi networks?

Answer:I would check if Wi-Fi is enabled, verify if the device is within range of a Wi-Fi network, and review system logs for any relevant error messages. Additionally, I might restart the Wi-Fi router.

2. Describe your approach to resolving issues with slow Wi-Fi speeds on macOS.

Answer:I would check for signal interference, optimize Wi-Fi channels, update Wi-Fi drivers, and inspect for other devices causing network congestion. Using tools like Wireless Diagnostics can provide additional insights.

3. What steps would you take to troubleshoot Wi-Fi connection drops on a macOS device?

Answer:I would update Wi-Fi drivers, adjust router settings, and use Wireless Diagnostics to identify potential interference or signal issues. Ensuring the device is within range of the Wi-Fi signal is also crucial.

DNS and Connectivity Issues:

1. How do you troubleshoot DNS resolution issues on macOS?

Answer:I would verify DNS server settings, try using alternative DNS servers, flush the DNS cache using the Terminal, and check for any system-wide DNS-related issues.

2. What steps would you take to troubleshoot a macOS device that can ping IP addresses but not resolve domain names?

Answer:I would check DNS settings, verify the DNS server's availability, and investigate potential issues with the system's hosts file. I might also review firewall settings.

3. How do you troubleshoot a macOS device experiencing intermittent loss of internet connectivity?

Answer:I would review system logs for any recurring issues, check network cables and connections, and use tools like Ping and traceroute to identify the source of the intermittent connectivity loss.

Firewall and Security Troubleshooting:

1. Discuss the steps you would take to troubleshoot firewall-related issues on macOS.

Answer:I would review firewall settings in "System Preferences," check for any third-party firewall software, and inspect system logs for firewall-related events. Ensuring necessary ports are open is also important.

2. How do you troubleshoot a macOS device that cannot establish a secure connection to a specific website?

Answer:I would check the website's SSL certificate, verify the device's date and time settings, and review any firewall or proxy settings that might be affecting secure connections.

3. Describe your approach to troubleshooting a macOS device experiencing unusual network activity or potential security threats.

Answer:I would use network monitoring tools, inspect logs for suspicious activity, and run antivirus and anti-malware scans. If necessary, I might isolate the device from the network for further analysis.

VPN and Connectivity Issues:

1. How would you troubleshoot VPN connectivity issues on a macOS device?

Answer:I would verify VPN settings, check for any conflicting network configurations, and inspect system logs for VPN-related errors. Updating VPN software and ensuring compatibility are also key steps.

2. What steps would you take to troubleshoot a macOS device that cannot connect to a specific VPN server?

Answer:I would verify the VPN server's availability, check for correct authentication details, and review VPN logs for any error messages. Ensuring the macOS device has the latest VPN client version is also important.

3. Discuss your approach to troubleshooting issues with a macOS device that experiences network connectivity problems specifically when connected to a VPN.

Answer:I would review split-tunneling settings, check for conflicts with other network configurations, and use network monitoring tools to identify any issues introduced by the VPN connection.

Command-Line Tools for Network Troubleshooting:

1. How do you use the ping command to troubleshoot network issues on macOS?

Answer:I would use ping to test the reachability of a host, identify packet loss, and determine latency. Analysing the output can provide insights into network health.

2. Explain the purpose of the traceroute command and how it can be used for network troubleshooting on macOS.

Answer:traceroute traces the route packets take to reach a destination, helping identify network hops and potential points of failure. It is useful for diagnosing connectivity issues.

3. How can the netstat command be utilized to troubleshoot network issues on macOS?

Answer:I would use netstat to view active network connections, identify listening ports, and inspect routing tables. Analyzing this information can help pinpoint network-related problems.

System Logs and Network Troubleshooting:

1. Where can you find relevant network-related information in macOS system logs, and how do you interpret this information?

Answer: System logs can be found in the Console app. I would look for entries related to network interfaces, DHCP, Wi-Fi, and firewall events. Analyzing timestamps and error messages is crucial.

2. How do you troubleshoot network issues by examining logs in the Console app on macOS?

Answer:I would filter logs based on network-related events, look for error messages or warnings, and use timestamps to correlate events. This can provide insights into the timing and nature of network issues.

3. Discuss the types of network-related events you might find in macOS logs and their significance for troubleshooting.

Answer: Events may include DHCP lease renewals, Wi-Fi connection drops, firewall activity, and network interface status changes. Understanding the context of these events aids in diagnosing issues.

Network Monitoring and Diagnostics:

1. How can network monitoring tools like Wireshark be used to troubleshoot network issues on macOS?

Answer:I would use Wireshark to capture and analyze network traffic, identify anomalies, and pinpoint the source of issues such as packet loss, latency, or unexpected traffic.

2. Describe your approach to using the Network Utility tool on macOS for troubleshooting network issues.

Answer: Network Utility provides tools like Ping, Traceroute, and Netstat. I would use these tools to test connectivity, trace network paths, and inspect active connections for troubleshooting purposes.

3. How can you use the Wireless Diagnostics tool on macOS to troubleshoot Wi-Fi issues?

Answer: Wireless Diagnostics provides information on Wi-Fi networks, interference, and signal strength. I would use it to identify potential Wi-Fi issues, such as interference or signal degradation.

Network Hardware and Device Configuration:

1. How do you troubleshoot network issues related to hardware, such as routers or switches?

Answer:I would check the status lights on network hardware, inspect cable connections, and review device logs if available. Additionally, updating firmware and checking for hardware failures is crucial.

2. Discuss your approach to troubleshooting network issues on a macOS device connected to a corporate network with complex configurations.

Answer:I would work closely with the IT team to understand network policies, security configurations, and potential conflicts. Analyzing logs and collaborating with network administrators is essential.

3. How can you troubleshoot a macOS device that cannot connect to a specific network printer?

Answer:I would check printer connectivity, verify printer settings, and ensure the macOS device has the necessary printer drivers installed. Inspecting system logs for any print-related errors is also important.

Security and Compliance:

1. How do you ensure network troubleshooting activities comply with security policies and protocols?

Answer:I would follow established security procedures, avoid using insecure diagnostic tools, and collaborate with security teams to ensure that troubleshooting activities align with organizational security standards.

2. Discuss your approach to troubleshooting network issues in a secure and sensitive environment, such as a financial institution or healthcare organization.

Answer:I would prioritize security, work within the constraints of compliance regulations, and ensure that network troubleshooting activities do not compromise sensitive data. Collaboration with security teams is crucial.

User Interaction and Communication:

1. How do you communicate network issues and resolutions to non-technical users or stakeholders?

Answer:I would use clear and non-technical language to explain the issue, its impact, and the steps taken for resolution. Providing updates throughout the troubleshooting process is important.

2. Discuss your approach to managing user expectations during the network troubleshooting process.

Answer:I would set realistic expectations regarding the timeline for resolution, keep users informed of progress, and provide clear instructions for any actions they need to take. Transparency is key.

Continuous Improvement and Documentation:

1. How do you ensure continuous improvement in network troubleshooting processes?

Answer:I regularly update my knowledge on network technologies, stay informed about emerging trends, and seek feedback from colleagues. Learning from each troubleshooting experience helps refine future approaches.

2. Discuss the importance of documentation in the network troubleshooting process, and how do you maintain comprehensive records?

Answer: Documentation is crucial for future reference and knowledge sharing. I maintain detailed records of troubleshooting steps, configurations, and resolutions, often using a combination of written notes and digital tools.

Collaboration and Teamwork:

1. How do you collaborate with other IT teams, such as system administrators or security professionals, when troubleshooting network issues?

Answer:I maintain open communication channels, share relevant information, and collaborate closely with other IT teams. Regular meetings and joint troubleshooting sessions facilitate effective teamwork.

2. Describe a situation where you had to work with external vendors or service providers to resolve a complex network issue on macOS.

Answer:I collaborated with a network equipment vendor to diagnose and resolve issues with a specific router model. Effective communication and sharing detailed diagnostic information were crucial in reaching a resolution.

Professional Development:

1. How do you stay informed about the latest developments and best practices in network troubleshooting for macOS?

Answer:I regularly participate in industry forums, attend relevant conferences, and engage in continuous learning through online courses and certifications. Networking with peers and staying informed about vendor updates are also part of my routine.

2. Discuss your long-term goals and aspirations related to network troubleshooting and IT management.

Answer: My long-term goals include further specialization in network security, obtaining advanced certifications, and contributing to the development of efficient and secure network infrastructure. I aspire to take on leadership roles in IT management and contribute to the strategic development of technology initiatives within organizations.

Security Considerations

General Security Knowledge:

1. What are the key security features in macOS?

Answer: macOS incorporates features such as Gatekeeper, XProtect, FileVault, and System Integrity Protection (SIP) to enhance security.

2. Explain the concept of sandboxing in macOS.

Answer: Sandboxing restricts the permissions and resources available to applications, enhancing security by limiting potential damage.

3. How does macOS handle encryption, and what is the role of FileVault?

Answer: FileVault is macOS's disk encryption program, securing data at rest by encrypting the entire disk.

4. Can you explain the purpose of System Integrity Protection (SIP) in macOS?

Answer: SIP protects critical system files and processes from being modified by even the root user, enhancing the integrity of the operating system.

5. What is Gatekeeper, and how does it contribute to macOS security?

Answer: Gatekeeper ensures that only signed and trusted applications can run on a Mac, reducing the risk of malware.

Authentication and Access Control:

1. How does macOS manage user authentication, and what role does Touch ID play?

Answer: macOS uses a combination of passwords and Touch ID for user authentication, providing a convenient and secure method for users to access their systems.

2. Explain the concept of multi-factor authentication in the context of macOS.

Answer: Multi-factor authentication on macOS typically involves a combination of something the user knows (password) and something the user has (e.g., a trusted device).

3. Can you discuss the role of Keychain in macOS security?

Answer: Keychain is a secure password manager on macOS, storing and managing user passwords and cryptographic keys.

4. How does macOS handle access control for applications and system resources?

Answer: macOS utilizes a combination of user permissions, access control lists (ACLs), and application sandboxing to control access to resources.

5. Explain how role-based access control (RBAC) is implemented in macOS.

Answer: RBAC in macOS involves assigning specific roles and permissions to users, allowing for fine-grained control over system access.

Network Security:

1. What are the key considerations for securing network communication on macOS?

Answer: Securing network communication on macOS involves using technologies such as firewalls, VPNs, and ensuring the use of secure protocols.

2. How does macOS address the threat of man-in-the-middle attacks?

Answer: macOS uses technologies like X.509 certificates and Transport Layer Security (TLS) to mitigate the risk of man-in-the-middle attacks.

3. Discuss the role of the built-in macOS firewall in network security.

Answer: The macOS firewall monitors and controls incoming and outgoing network traffic, providing an additional layer of protection against unauthorized access.

4. How can you secure Wi-Fi connections on macOS?

Answer: Securing Wi-Fi connections involves using strong encryption (e.g., WPA2 or WPA3) and disabling unnecessary services like WPS.

5. Can you explain how Virtual Private Networks (VPNs) enhance network security on macOS?

Answer: VPNs on macOS encrypt internet traffic, providing a secure and private connection, especially when using untrusted networks.

Threat Detection and Response:

1. What tools and techniques can be used for malware detection on macOS?

Answer: macOS employs XProtect and Gatekeeper for real-time malware detection, supplemented by third-party antivirus solutions.

2. How does macOS handle security vulnerabilities and software updates?

Answer: macOS regularly releases software updates to patch security vulnerabilities, and users are encouraged to keep their systems up-to-date.

3. Discuss the importance of log analysis in macOS security.

Answer: Log analysis helps in identifying potential security incidents by reviewing system and application logs for abnormal activities.

4. How can you respond to a security incident on a macOS system?

Answer: A response plan may involve isolating affected systems, analyzing logs, applying patches, and restoring from backups.

5. Explain the role of incident response planning in macOS security.

Answer: Incident response planning involves preparing for and efficiently addressing security incidents, minimizing the impact on the organization.

Cryptography and Secure Communication:

1. How does macOS ensure secure communication over the internet?

Answer: Secure communication is achieved through the use of protocols like HTTPS, TLS, and encrypted connections for email (e.g., S/MIME).

2. Discuss the use of certificates in macOS for secure communication.

Answer: Certificates, managed by Keychain, are used to establish the authenticity of websites and encrypt communication.

3. Can you explain how FileVault contributes to the security of data at rest?

Answer: FileVault uses XTS-AES-128 encryption to secure the data on the startup disk, protecting it from unauthorized access.

4. How does macOS handle the generation and management of cryptographic keys?

Answer: macOS uses Keychain and the CoreCrypto framework for secure key management and generation.

5. Discuss the role of Secure Sockets Layer (SSL) and Transport Layer Security (TLS) in macOS security.

Answer: SSL and TLS are cryptographic protocols used to secure communication over networks, including web browsing and email.

Application Security:

1. How does macOS handle code signing, and why is it important?

Answer: Code signing ensures that applications on macOS are from legitimate sources and haven't been tampered with, enhancing security.

2. Explain the process of app notarization in macOS.

Answer: App notarization is a step where Apple checks and confirms the security of an app before it is distributed, reducing the risk of malicious software.

3. Can you discuss the security considerations for developing and deploying Mac App Store applications?

Answer: Mac App Store applications must adhere to strict security guidelines to ensure user safety and maintain the integrity of the platform.

4. How does macOS protect against privilege escalation vulnerabilities in applications?

Answer: macOS employs mechanisms like sandboxing and code signing to prevent privilege escalation attacks.

5. Discuss the role of the Apple Developer Program in maintaining app security on macOS.

Answer: The Apple Developer Program provides tools and resources to developers, ensuring that their apps meet security standards before distribution.

Endpoint Security:

1. What are the key components of endpoint security on macOS?

Answer: Endpoint security on macOS involves antivirus software, firewalls, intrusion detection systems, and secure configuration settings.

2. How does macOS address the security challenges of removable media (e.g., USB drives)?

Answer: macOS prompts users for permission before executing actions related to removable media, reducing the risk of malware.

3. Discuss the importance of strong password policies in macOS security.

Answer: Strong password policies, including length and complexity requirements, are crucial for protecting user accounts on macOS systems.

4. How can you enforce security policies on macOS devices in an enterprise environment?

Answer: Tools like Mobile Device Management (MDM) solutions can be used to enforce security policies, manage configurations, and monitor devices.

5. Explain the role of Secure Boot in ensuring the integrity of the macOS startup process.

Answer: Secure Boot ensures that only signed and authorized firmware and operating system software are loaded during the startup process.

Security Auditing and Compliance:

1. What are the key steps in conducting a security audit for macOS systems?

Answer: Security audits involve reviewing configurations, analyzing logs, conducting vulnerability assessments, and ensuring compliance with security policies.

2. How does macOS comply with industry standards for information security?

Answer: macOS adheres to standards such as Common Criteria, FIPS 140-2, and follows best practices outlined by organizations like NIST.

3. Discuss the role of penetration testing in assessing the security of macOS environments.

Answer: Penetration testing involves simulating cyberattacks to identify vulnerabilities and weaknesses in macOS systems.

4. How does macOS handle privacy considerations, especially with user data?

Answer: macOS prioritizes user privacy through features like App Tracking Transparency and privacy labels for App Store apps.

5. Can you discuss the challenges and solutions in maintaining security for legacy macOS systems?

Answer: Legacy systems may have vulnerabilities, and maintaining security involves a combination of patching, isolation, and migration to more secure platforms.

ONLINE RESOURCES

Practice PaperLink: https://forms.gle/dmGRvFkGDNPcGXcA6

QR Code:

Video Link:https://www.youtube.com/playlist?list=PLzlh_31VWEFoy5NPlWesJulwbo6LTGwHq

QR Code:

Chapter 9: mac OS System Maintenance

Disk Management and Optimization

Disk Management Fundamentals:

1. What is the role of Disk Utility in macOS, and how do you use it for disk management?

Answer: Disk Utility is a macOS tool for managing disks and storage. It can be used for partitioning, formatting, and repairing disks.

2. Explain the difference between APFS (Apple File System) and HFS+ (Mac OS Extended) in terms of disk management.

Answer:APFS is the newer, more advanced file system, providing features like snapshots and improved optimization over HFS+.

3. How does macOS handle disk encryption, and what is the significance of FileVault?

Answer: FileVault is macOS's disk encryption feature that secures data on the startup disk. It uses XTS-AES-128 encryption.

4. Discuss the considerations for choosing between different disk formats when formatting a disk.

Answer: Considerations include compatibility with other systems, performance requirements, and support for macOS features.

5. Can you explain the purpose of Fusion Drive in macOS and how it optimizes disk storage?

Answer: Fusion Drive combines SSD and HDD to provide a balance between speed and storage capacity, automatically moving frequently used files to the SSD.

Disk Partitioning and Formatting:

1. What factors should be considered when deciding on the number and size of partitions on a disk?

Answer: Considerations include the type of data, the need for multiple operating systems, and optimizing for performance.

2. Explain the process of resizing a disk partition in macOS without data loss.

Answer: Disk Utility can be used to resize partitions, but it's crucial to have a backup in case of unexpected issues.

3. How does macOS handle the mounting and unmounting of external storage devices?

Answer: External storage devices are automatically mounted when connected and can be unmounted using Disk Utility or the command line.

4. Discuss the advantages and disadvantages of using the APFS format over HFS+ for disk partitions.

Answer:APFS offers improved performance, snapshots, and encryption but may not be compatible with older macOS versions.

5. Can you explain the role of the Master Boot Record (MBR) and GUID Partition Table (GPT) in disk partitioning on macOS?

Answer:MBR and GPT are partitioning schemes. macOS typically uses GPT for modern systems due to its advantages in handling large disks.

Disk Optimization Techniques:

1. What strategies can be employed to optimize disk performance on a Mac?

Answer: Techniques include minimizing file fragmentation, using SSDs for improved speed, and managing startup items.

2. Discuss the impact of disk fragmentation on macOS performance and how it can be addressed.

Answer: Fragmentation can slow down file access. macOS automatically defragments small files, but for larger files, tools like iDefrag can be used.

3. How can you identify and address disk space issues on a macOS system?

Answer: Tools like Disk Utility and third-party applications help identify large files and free up disk space by removing unnecessary files.

4. Explain how TRIM support in macOS contributes to the optimization of SSDs.

Answer:TRIM support helps maintain the performance of SSDs by proactively managing the storage blocks.

5. What role does the purge command play in optimizing system performance, especially concerning disk usage?

Answer: The purge command frees up inactive memory, potentially improving system performance by reducing the need for swapping to disk.

Backup and Recovery:

1. Discuss the importance of regular backups for disk management and optimization.

Answer: Regular backups are crucial for data recovery in case of hardware failures, data corruption, or accidental deletions.

2. How can Time Machine be utilized for effective backup and recovery on macOS?

Answer: Time Machine is an automatic backup tool that creates incremental backups, allowing users to restore their system to a previous state.

3. Explain the considerations when choosing an external drive for Time Machine backups.

Answer: The external drive should have sufficient capacity, support macOS formats, and ideally be connected via a fast interface like Thunderbolt or USB 3.0.

4. What steps can be taken to ensure the security of backup data stored on external drives?

Answer: Encrypting Time Machine backups adds an extra layer of security, preventing unauthorized access to the backup data.

5. In the event of a disk failure, how would you approach the recovery process using Time Machine?

Answer: Replace the failed disk, reinstall macOS, and use Time Machine to restore the system to its previous state.

Disk Monitoring and Maintenance:

1. How can you monitor disk health and performance on a macOS system?

Answer: Tools like Disk Utility, Disk Utility's First Aid, and third-party applications such as DriveDx can be used for disk monitoring.

2. Discuss the significance of S.M.A.R.T. (Self-Monitoring, Analysis and Reporting Technology) in monitoring disk health.

Answer:S.M.A.R.T. provides real-time monitoring of disk health, helping predict and prevent disk failures.

3. Explain the purpose of the macOS Disk Utility's First Aid feature and how it contributes to disk maintenance.

Answer: First Aid checks and repairs file system issues, helping maintain the integrity and health of the disk.

4. How can you optimize disk performance by managing startup items on macOS?

Answer: Limiting unnecessary startup items can reduce the load on the system, resulting in faster boot times and improved performance.

5. Can you discuss the role of periodic disk cleanup in maintaining macOS system performance?

Answer: Regularly cleaning up unnecessary files, caches, and temporary data helps free up disk space and can contribute to improved performance.

Command Line and Automation:

1. How can Terminal commands be used for disk management tasks on macOS?

Answer: Commands like diskutil, df, and diskutil apfs resizeContainer can be used for various disk-related tasks.

2. Discuss the advantages of using the command line for disk management over graphical tools.

Answer: The command line provides more flexibility, scripting capabilities, and can be used in remote or headless environments.

3. How can you automate disk maintenance tasks on macOS using scripts or third-party tools?

Answer: Tools like cron or launchd can schedule scripts for automated disk maintenance tasks, ensuring regular optimization.

4. Explain the use of the rsync command for efficient data transfer and synchronization between disks.

Answer:rsync is a powerful command for synchronizing files and directories between disks, ensuring data consistency.

5. Discuss the use of disk cloning as a strategy for backup and system recovery.

Answer: Disk cloning involves creating an exact copy of a disk, which can be useful for backup and restoring systems to a previous state.

Advanced Disk Management Topics:

1. What is the role of RAID (Redundant Array of Independent Disks) in macOS, and how does it contribute to disk optimization?

Answer:RAID configurations can enhance performance, reliability, or a combination of both by combining multiple disks into a single logical unit.

2. Discuss the considerations and steps involved in migrating data from an HDD to an SSD on a macOS system.

Answer: Migrating from HDD to SSD involves cloning the disk, updating settings for optimal SSD performance, and ensuring TRIM support.

3. How can you troubleshoot and address issues related to external drives not mounting on a macOS system?

Answer: Troubleshooting involves checking cables, using Disk Utility to mount the drive, and ensuring compatibility with the macOS version.

4. Explain the process of creating and managing disk images on macOS.

Answer: Disk images are virtual disks stored in a file. Disk Utility can be used to create, mount, and manage disk images.

5. Discuss the considerations for implementing disk quotas on macOS in a multi-user environment.

Answer: Disk quotas help manage disk space usage for individual users, preventing one user from consuming all available space.

Security Considerations in Disk Management:

1. How does disk encryption, particularly FileVault, contribute to overall system security in macOS?

Answer: Disk encryption protects data at rest, preventing unauthorized access even if the physical disk is compromised.

2. Can you explain how macOS handles secure erasure of data on SSDs, considering wear leveling and TRIM support?

Answer: Securely erasing data on SSDs involves sending a secure erase command, which is managed by the SSD's firmware and TRIM support.

3. Discuss the role of permissions and access control in securing data on macOS disks.

Answer: Permissions control which users can access and modify data on a disk, providing a layer of security.

4. How can you address security concerns when disposing of or selling a macOS system with an SSD?

Answer: Securely erasing the SSD and reinstalling macOS ensures that sensitive data is not accessible to the new owner.

5. In a scenario where a macOS system has been compromised, what steps would you take to secure and recover data from the affected disk?

Answer: Isolate the compromised system, perform a security audit, and restore data from a clean backup to ensure a secure and clean state.

Backup and Restore Strategies

Backup Strategies and Planning:

1. Why is having a robust backup strategy crucial for macOS systems?

Answer:A robust backup strategy is essential to protect against data loss due to hardware failure, software issues, or accidental deletions.

2. Explain the difference between local and remote backups. What factors influence the choice between them?

Answer: Local backups are stored on a physical device, while remote backups are stored on a different network or cloud service. The choice depends on factors like data security, accessibility, and disaster recovery planning.

3. How do you determine the frequency of backups for a macOS system, and what factors influence this decision?

Answer: Backup frequency depends on the criticality of data, the frequency of changes, and the acceptable data loss in the event of a failure. Regular assessments help fine-tune backup schedules.

4. Can you discuss the considerations when selecting backup storage media (e.g., external drives, NAS, cloud)?

Answer: Factors include storage capacity, speed, cost, and the level of accessibility required for backup storage.

5. Explain the concept of a 3-2-1 backup strategy, and why is it considered a best practice?

Answer: The 3-2-1 strategy involves having three copies of data, stored on two different media, with one copy stored offsite. It provides redundancy and protection against various failure scenarios.

Time Machine and System Restore:

1. How does Time Machine work, and what are its advantages and limitations?

Answer: Time Machine is an automatic backup feature that creates incremental backups, allowing users to restore their system to a specific point in time. It provides an easy-to-use interface but may lack advanced customization options.

2. Discuss the steps involved in setting up and configuring Time Machine on a macOS system.

Answer: Setting up Time Machine involves selecting a backup disk and configuring preferences such as backup frequency and exclusions.

3. What role does the Time Machine local snapshot feature play in macOS backups?

Answer: Local snapshots allow Time Machine to create backups even when the backup disk is not connected, providing additional protection against data loss.

4. Can you explain how the System Restore feature in macOS works, and when would you use it?

Answer: System Restore allows users to roll back their system to a previous state. It is useful when troubleshooting issues caused by recent changes or updates.

5. How can you customize Time Machine settings to exclude specific files or folders from backups?

Answer: In Time Machine preferences, you can add items to the exclusion list to prevent them from being included in backups.

Backup Encryption and Security:

1. Why is encrypting backup data important, and how does macOS handle encryption for Time Machine backups?

Answer: Encrypting backup data ensures the confidentiality of sensitive information. Time Machine offers the option to encrypt backups with FileVault.

2. Discuss the security considerations when using cloud-based backup solutions for macOS.

Answer: Cloud-based backup solutions should use secure transmission (e.g., SSL), encrypt data at rest, and comply with industry standards for data security.

3. How can you ensure the security of Time Machine backups stored on an external drive?

Answer: Encrypting Time Machine backups with FileVault provides an additional layer of security, ensuring that the backup data is protected.

4. In a corporate environment, how would you address security concerns related to backing up sensitive data on macOS?

Answer: Implementing encryption, access controls, and regular security audits can help address security concerns in a corporate backup strategy.

5. Can you explain the role of key management in backup encryption, especially in enterprise-level macOS environments?

Answer: Key management involves securely managing encryption keys, ensuring that only authorized individuals can access backup data.

Backup Monitoring and Verification:

1. How do you monitor the success and health of Time Machine backups on macOS?

Answer: Time Machine provides notifications for successful and unsuccessful backups. Additionally, tools like Console can be used for more detailed logs.

2. Discuss the importance of periodic backup testing and verification in macOS environments.

Answer: Testing backups ensures that the data can be successfully restored, verifying the integrity of the backup process.

3. What steps can you take to troubleshoot and resolve issues with failed Time Machine backups?

Answer: Troubleshooting involves checking disk integrity, reviewing system logs, and ensuring the backup disk has sufficient space.

4. How can you verify the integrity of data in a Time Machine backup without restoring it?

Answer: The tmutil compare command can be used to compare the current state of the system with the Time Machine backup without performing a full restore.

5. Explain the role of backup reporting tools in macOS backup strategies, and provide examples.

Answer: Backup reporting tools provide insights into the success and status of backups. Examples include Time Machine Buddy and third-party monitoring solutions.

Disaster Recovery Planning:

1. What considerations should be taken into account when creating a disaster recovery plan for macOS systems?

Answer:A disaster recovery plan should include procedures for system restoration, backup testing, and documentation of critical information.

2. How would you approach the restoration of a macOS system after a catastrophic failure?

Answer: Restore macOS by reinstalling the operating system, using Time Machine or other backups to recover data and settings.

3. Discuss the importance of documenting backup and restore procedures in a disaster recovery plan.

Answer: Documentation ensures that recovery procedures are well-defined and can be executed efficiently in high-stress situations.

4. In a scenario where a macOS system needs to be replaced, what steps would you take to migrate data and settings?

Answer: Use Time Machine or migration tools during the initial macOS setup to transfer data and settings from the old system to the new one.

5. How do you balance the need for quick recovery with the importance of thorough data verification during a restore process?

Answer: Prioritize quick recovery for critical systems while ensuring that thorough data verification is performed during less time-sensitive scenarios.

Third-Party Backup Solutions:

1. Can you discuss the advantages and limitations of using third-party backup solutions for macOS compared to Time Machine?

Answer: Third-party solutions may offer additional features, customization options, and compatibility with different storage solutions but may come at an additional cost.

2. Provide examples of third-party backup solutions for macOS, and discuss their unique features.

Answer: Examples include Carbon Copy Cloner, SuperDuper!, and Acronis True Image. They often offer features like disk cloning, incremental backups, and scheduling.

3. How would you approach the integration of a third-party backup solution into an existing macOS backup strategy?

Answer: Integrate third-party solutions by considering compatibility, adjusting backup schedules, and ensuring that it aligns with the overall backup strategy.

4. Discuss the role of cloud-based backup solutions in macOS environments and potential considerations when choosing a provider.

Answer: Cloud-based solutions offer offsite storage and accessibility. Considerations include data security, cost, and the provider's reputation.

5. How can you ensure that third-party backup solutions adhere to industry standards and compliance requirements for data security?

Answer: Choose solutions that provide encryption options, comply with industry standards, and undergo regular security audits.

Command Line and Scripting for Backups:

1. How can you perform manual backups using command-line tools on macOS, and what are the advantages of this approach?

Answer: Tools like rsync and tar can be used for manual backups, providing flexibility and scripting capabilities.

2. Discuss the use of cron or launchd for scheduling automated backups using command-line tools on macOS.

Answer: These scheduling tools allow for the automation of backup scripts, ensuring regular and consistent backups.

3. How would you approach scripting for backup verification and reporting in a macOS environment?

Answer: Scripts can be written to compare backup data with the current system state and generate reports for monitoring and verification purposes.

4. In what scenarios would you use the tmutil command for Time Machine-related tasks, and provide examples.

Answer: tmutil can be used for tasks such as enabling Time Machine, managing exclusions, and triggering manual backups.

5. Explain the use of ditto command for creating and restoring backups in macOS.

Answer: The ditto command copies files and directories, making it suitable for creating backups or restoring data.

Scalability and Enterprise-Level Backup:

1. How do backup strategies differ when managing data for a large enterprise versus a small business or individual?

Answer: Enterprise-level strategies involve scalability, centralized management, and the integration of backup solutions with other enterprise systems.

2. Discuss the role of data deduplication in enterprise-level backup solutions and its impact on storage efficiency.

Answer: Data deduplication eliminates redundant data, reducing the storage space required for backups in an enterprise environment.

3. How can you ensure that backup and restore processes in an enterprise environment align with compliance requirements?

Answer: Implement backup solutions that support compliance standards, perform regular audits, and document adherence to compliance requirements.

4. In an enterprise setting, how would you design a backup strategy to accommodate multiple macOS devices across different locations?

Answer: Implement a centralized backup solution, potentially using network-attached storage (NAS) or cloud-based solutions, and ensure secure and efficient data transmission.

5. What role does automation play in managing backups at an enterprise scale, and how can it improve efficiency?

Answer: Automation streamlines backup processes, reduces the risk of human error, and ensures consistent and timely execution of backups across a large number of systems.

System Monitoring and Performance Tuning

System Monitoring:

1. Explain the importance of system monitoring in macOS.

Answer: System monitoring is crucial for identifying performance bottlenecks, resource utilization, and potential issues. It helps ensure optimal system performance and proactively addresses any anomalies.

2. What macOS tools do you use for real-time system monitoring, and how do they work?

Answer: Tools like Activity Monitor and command-line utilities like top and vm_stat provide real-time insights into CPU, memory, disk, and network usage.

3. How do you set up custom alerts for specific system metrics in macOS?

Answer: Use tools like cron jobs combined with scripts or third-party monitoring solutions to set up custom alerts based on predefined thresholds.

4. Explain the role of logs in system monitoring on macOS.

Answer: Logs, found in /var/log, are essential for diagnosing issues. Console and syslog provide valuable information about system events, errors, and warnings.

5. Describe the process of analysing system logs to troubleshoot performance issues.

Answer: Use Console to filter logs based on relevant timeframes and search for error messages or patterns that may indicate performance issues.

6. How would you monitor disk I/O in macOS, and what tools would you use?

Answer: Disk Utility and iostat are useful for monitoring disk I/O. Analyze read and write rates, as well as disk latency, to assess performance.

7. What are the key considerations when monitoring network performance on a macOS system?

Answer: Use tools like netstat and Activity Monitor to track network usage, check for unusual activity, and identify potential network-related issues.

Performance Tuning:

1. Explain the importance of performance tuning in macOS.

Answer: Performance tuning involves optimizing system resources to improve efficiency, responsiveness, and overall system performance.

2. How do you identify CPU-bound processes on a macOS system?

Answer: Tools like Activity Monitor and top can help identify processes with high CPU usage. Analyze these processes to understand and address the cause.

3. Describe the steps you would take to optimize memory usage on a macOS system.

Answer: Identify memory-hungry processes using Activity Monitor, optimize applications, and consider upgrading RAM if necessary.

4. What is the role of swap space in macOS, and how can you optimize its usage?

Answer: Swap space is used when physical memory is exhausted. Monitor swap usage with tools like vm_stat and optimize by reducing memory-intensive processes.

5. How do you analyze disk performance issues on a macOS system, and what optimizations can be applied?

Answer: Use tools like iostat to identify disk bottlenecks. Optimize by addressing unnecessary background processes, upgrading to an SSD, or adjusting disk configurations.

6. Explain the concept of kernel tuning in macOS and provide examples of parameters that can be tuned.

Answer: Kernel tuning involves adjusting kernel parameters for better performance. Examples include adjusting TCP/IP settings or file system parameters using sysctl.

7. What techniques would you employ to optimize network performance on a macOS system?

Answer: Optimize network performance by addressing DNS issues, adjusting TCP window sizes, and considering Quality of Service (QoS) configurations.

Advanced Concepts:

1. Describe your experience with DTrace and how it can be used for performance analysis on macOS.

Answer:DTrace is a dynamic tracing framework. Use it to analyze system activity, profile applications, and troubleshoot performance issues.

2. Explain the role of XNU in macOS and its impact on system performance.

Answer:XNU is the macOS kernel. Understanding its architecture is crucial for advanced performance tuning and troubleshooting.

3. How would you approach performance tuning for graphics-intensive applications on a macOS system?

Answer: Optimize graphics performance by updating graphics drivers, adjusting system preferences, and optimizing the application's rendering pipeline.

4. Discuss your experience with macOS server performance tuning and monitoring.

Answer: Server performance tuning involves optimizing services, adjusting server parameters, and monitoring resource usage. Tools like Server.app and command-line utilities are used.

5. Describe your experience with virtualization and its impact on macOS system performance.

Answer: Virtualization introduces additional layers. Considerations include allocating appropriate resources, optimizing virtual machine configurations, and monitoring performance within virtual environments.

6. How would you handle performance tuning for macOS systems in a clustered or distributed environment?

Answer: Considerations include load balancing, optimizing network communication, and ensuring uniform resource distribution across the cluster.

ONLINE RESOURCES

Practice Paper Link: https://forms.gle/6uihVAdK4eM4BDM1A

QR Code:

Video Link: https://www.youtube.com/playlist?list=PLzlh_31VWEFptNJTD-9dKfvCEdDU8Jxyd

QR Code:

Chapter 10: mac OS Troubleshooting Techniques

Common Mac Issues and Solutions

General Mac Issues:

1. What steps would you take to troubleshoot a Mac that won't boot?

Answer: Start with safe mode, check startup disk integrity using Disk Utility, and troubleshoot hardware components.

2. How do you address kernel panic issues on a Mac?

Answer: Review panic logs using Console, update drivers, and check for hardware issues. Kernel panics may also result from incompatible software or corrupt system files.

3. Explain how you would troubleshoot a Mac experiencing frequent application crashes.

Answer: Check for software updates, isolate problematic applications, and review crash logs to identify the root cause.

4. What steps do you take when a Mac is running slow?

Answer: Check Activity Monitor for resource-hungry processes, optimize startup items, clear cache files, and consider hardware upgrades if necessary.

5. How would you address Wi-Fi connectivity issues on a Mac?

Answer: Reset network settings, update Wi-Fi drivers, check for interference, and ensure the correct network configuration.

6. Explain the process of troubleshooting Bluetooth connectivity problems on a Mac.

Answer: Verify device compatibility, update Bluetooth drivers, reset Bluetooth preferences, and check for interference.

7. What steps would you take to resolve a Mac with a frozen or unresponsive application?

Answer: Use Force Quit to close the application, check for updates, and analyze crash logs to identify potential issues.

Hardware and Peripheral Issues:

1. How do you troubleshoot issues with a Mac not recognizing external devices like USB drives or printers?

Answer: Check cable connections, test devices on other computers, update drivers, and verify compatibility.

2. Explain the steps you would take to address a Mac with a malfunctioning keyboard or trackpad.

Answer: Check for physical damage, clean input devices, update macOS, and reset System Management Controller (SMC).

3. What would you do if a Mac is not recognizing or charging the battery properly?

Answer: Verify the power adapter and cable, reset SMC, and check battery health using System Report.

4. How do you troubleshoot display-related issues on a Mac?

Answer: Check cable connections, update graphics drivers, adjust display settings, and run diagnostics for hardware issues.

5. What steps would you take if a Mac is overheating?

Answer: Check for dust accumulation, optimize airflow, monitor CPU usage, and consider hardware upgrades if needed.

Software and Operating System Issues:

1. How do you address issues with macOS updates failing to install?

Answer: Check available disk space, verify internet connectivity, and consider manually downloading and installing the update.

2. What steps would you take to troubleshoot software conflicts causing instability in macOS?

Answer: Identify conflicting software, check for updates, and use Safe Mode to isolate third-party software issues.

3. How do you resolve issues with Time Machine backups failing or not completing successfully?

Answer: Check backup disk integrity, review Time Machine preferences, and address disk space limitations.

4. What steps do you take when macOS applications are not responding or hanging?

Answer: Use Force Quit to close unresponsive applications, check for updates, and analyze crash reports for potential solutions.

5. Explain how you would troubleshoot and resolve issues with the macOS login process.

Answer: Resetting the login keychain, verifying user credentials, and checking for corrupted system files are common troubleshooting steps.

Security and Malware Issues:

1. How do you address a Mac infected with malware or adware?

Answer: Use reliable antivirus software, manually remove suspicious applications, and reset browser settings.

2. What steps would you take to secure a Mac and protect it from potential security threats?

Answer: Enable FileVault for disk encryption, keep software up to date, use a standard user account, and install reputable antivirus software.

3. How do you troubleshoot issues with Gatekeeper blocking the installation of certain applications?

Answer: Adjust Gatekeeper settings, check for developer signatures, and ensure the application comes from a reputable source.

Networking and Internet Issues:

1. How would you troubleshoot a Mac with intermittent or slow internet connectivity?

Answer: Check router settings, reset network configurations, and use Network Utility to diagnose connectivity issues.

2. What steps do you take when a Mac is unable to connect to a specific Wi-Fi network?

Answer: Forget and rejoin the network, check for MAC address filtering, and ensure the correct Wi-Fi password is used.

3. How do you address issues with a Mac unable to obtain an IP address via DHCP?

Answer: Verify router settings, reset DHCP lease, and manually configure network settings if needed.

Advanced Troubleshooting:

1. Explain your experience with Single User Mode and how it can be used for advanced troubleshooting.

Answer: Single User Mode provides a command-line interface for troubleshooting, repairing disk issues, and performing advanced diagnostics.

2. How would you approach troubleshooting issues with macOS networking in a multi-subnet environment?

Answer: Consider routing configurations, check DNS settings, and analyze firewall rules for inter-subnet communication.

3. Describe your experience with macOS Recovery mode and its role in system troubleshooting.

Answer: Recovery mode allows for disk repair, reinstallation of macOS, and restoring from Time Machine backups. It is essential for system recovery.

4. What steps do you take to troubleshoot issues with a Mac experiencing frequent system freezes or hangs?

Answer: Analyze system logs for patterns, check for hardware issues, and use diagnostic tools to identify the root cause.

Data Management and File System Issues:

1. How do you troubleshoot issues with a Mac not recognizing an external hard drive?

Answer: Check cable connections, test on other systems, and use Disk Utility to verify the external drive's integrity.

2. Explain how you would address file system corruption issues on a Mac.

Answer: Use Disk Utility to repair disk permissions and verify disk integrity. More severe cases may require the use of fsck in Single User Mode.

3. What steps do you take to recover data from a Mac with a failing hard drive?

Answer: Use data recovery software, consider professional services, and avoid further use of the drive to prevent additional data loss.

4. How do you troubleshoot issues with a Mac not recognizing a Time Machine backup disk?

Answer: Verify disk compatibility, check disk integrity, and ensure the backup disk is properly connected and accessible.

Updates and Maintenance:

1. How would you approach troubleshooting issues with a Mac experiencing problems after a recent macOS update?

Answer: Check for compatibility issues with third-party software, review system logs, and consider rolling back the update if necessary.

2. What steps do you take to ensure a smooth macOS update process for a fleet of enterprise Macs?

Answer: Test updates in a controlled environment, monitor for issues, and create a rollback plan in case of unexpected problems.

3. Explain how you would optimize a Mac for long-term performance and stability.

Answer: Regularly update macOS, monitor resource usage, clean up unnecessary files, and perform routine maintenance tasks such as disk verification and repair.

Backup and Restore:

1. How do you troubleshoot issues with Time Machine backups not completing successfully?

Answer: Check backup disk integrity, ensure sufficient disk space, and review Time Machine preferences for errors.

2. What steps do you take to restore a Mac from a Time Machine backup?

Answer: Boot into macOS Recovery, choose "Restore from Time Machine Backup," and follow the on-screen instructions.

3. Explain your experience with macOS Migration Assistant and how it can be used for system recovery.

Answer: Migration Assistant is used for transferring data from one Mac to another. It's useful for migrating user accounts, applications, and files during system recovery.

User Account Management:

1. How would you troubleshoot issues with a user account unable to log in on a Mac?

Answer: Verify account credentials, reset the user's password, and check for disk space limitations that may prevent login.

2. What steps do you take to troubleshoot issues with a user account experiencing file access permissions problems?

Answer: Use the "Get Info" option to adjust file permissions, run Disk Utility to repair disk permissions, and consider creating a new user account if issues persist.

3. Explain your experience with managing macOS user profiles and preferences.

Answer: Managing user profiles involves customizing user preferences, configuring login items, and ensuring a consistent user experience across multiple Macs.

Diagnostic Tools and Logs

Diagnostic Tools:

1. Explain the purpose of the Activity Monitor in macOS and how it can be used for system diagnostics.

Answer: Activity Monitor provides real-time information about system resources. It helps diagnose issues by monitoring CPU, memory, disk, and network usage.

2. How do you use Console.app for troubleshooting on macOS?

Answer: Console.app displays system logs, crash reports, and other diagnostic messages. It helps identify issues and track events across the system.

3. Describe your experience with the macOS Terminal and how it is used for diagnostics.

Answer: Terminal provides a command-line interface. I use it for running diagnostic commands, analyzing logs, and performing advanced system configurations.

4. Explain the purpose of the Network Utility tool in macOS and how it can assist in diagnostics.

Answer: Network Utility helps diagnose network-related issues by providing information on network connections, DNS resolution, and other network parameters.

5. How do you use the Disk Utility tool for diagnostic purposes in macOS?

Answer: Disk Utility checks and repairs disk permissions, verifies and repairs disk integrity, and can be used to partition and format disks.

6. Describe your experience with the macOS built-in diagnostic tool, Apple Hardware Test.

Answer: Apple Hardware Test helps identify hardware issues by running diagnostic tests on the Mac's components. It's useful for troubleshooting potential hardware failures.

7. Explain how the Console in Xcode can be used for advanced macOS diagnostics.

Answer: Xcode's Console allows for real-time debugging and monitoring of applications. It's particularly useful for developers and advanced users for debugging issues.

8. What is the purpose of the Migration Assistant, and how can it be used for diagnostic scenarios?

Answer: Migration Assistant assists in transferring data between Macs. In diagnostic scenarios, it can be used to migrate user accounts and data to a new system.

Log Analysis:

1. How do you access and interpret system logs on macOS for troubleshooting?

Answer: System logs are found in /var/log. I use Console or Terminal to view logs, looking for error messages, warnings, or patterns indicating issues.

2. Explain the role of the Unified Logs in macOS and how they differ from traditional system logs.

Answer: Unified Logs are a centralized logging system introduced in macOS. They provide a structured and more efficient way to store and retrieve logs compared to traditional log files.

3. How would you troubleshoot a Mac issue using information from kernel logs?

Answer: Kernel logs, accessible via Console or Terminal, contain information about low-level system events. I analyze these logs to identify issues at the core of the operating system.

4. Describe your approach to analyzing application-specific logs for troubleshooting.

Answer: Applications often have their own log files. I review these logs using Console or text editors to identify patterns, errors, or events related to the specific application.

5. What is the significance of crash reports, and how do you analyze them to diagnose application issues?

Answer: Crash reports provide detailed information about the state of an application when it crashes. I analyze stack traces and error messages to pinpoint the cause of the crash.

6. How do you troubleshoot issues related to permissions by analyzing log files on macOS?

Answer:I review logs for permission-related errors or warnings. Tools like Console or analyzing system logs in Terminal help identify permission issues affecting system or application functionality.

Performance Monitoring:

1. Explain your experience with using vm_stat for performance monitoring on macOS.

Answer: vm_stat provides information about virtual memory usage. I use it to monitor page-ins, page-outs, and other metrics to assess memory performance.

2. How do you interpret and use data from the iostat command for disk performance analysis on macOS?

Answer: iostat displays input/output statistics for disks. I analyze metrics like disk throughput and response time to identify performance bottlenecks.

3. Describe your experience using top command for real-time monitoring of processes and system resources.

Answer: The top command provides real-time information about CPU and memory usage. I use it to identify resource-intensive processes and assess overall system performance.

4. How do you monitor network performance using netstat on macOS?

Answer: netstat displays network statistics. I use it to check active network connections, routing tables, and interface statistics to troubleshoot network issues.

5. Explain your approach to using the sysdiagnose command for collecting system diagnostic information.

Answer: sysdiagnose collects a comprehensive set of diagnostic information. I use it when troubleshooting complex issues, and it provides a detailed snapshot of the system's state.

Advanced Diagnostic Tools:

1. Describe your experience using DTrace for advanced system diagnostics on macOS.

Answer: DTrace is a dynamic tracing framework. I use it for in-depth analysis of system and application behavior, allowing for advanced performance tuning and troubleshooting.

2. How do you use Instruments in Xcode for profiling and performance analysis on macOS?

Answer: Instruments is a profiling and performance analysis tool. I use it to monitor CPU, memory, disk, and network usage during the execution of an application.

3. Explain your experience with using Wireshark for network packet analysis on macOS.

Answer: Wireshark is a network protocol analyzer. I use it to capture and analyze network packets, helping to diagnose complex network issues.

4. Describe your experience with the fs_usage command for monitoring file system activity.

Answer: fs_usage provides real-time file system activity information. I use it to track file operations, helping diagnose issues related to file access and modification.

5. How do you use the spindump command for diagnosing application responsiveness issues on macOS?

Answer: spindump captures and analyzes application thread traces. I use it to identify performance bottlenecks and diagnose issues related to application responsiveness.

Integration with Apple Ecosystem:

1. Explain the role of the Apple Diagnostics tool and how it differs from other diagnostic tools.

Answer: Apple Diagnostics is a hardware diagnostic tool built into Macs. It performs basic hardware tests and helps identify hardware-related issues.

2. How would you use the System Information tool for gathering comprehensive information about a Mac's hardware and software configuration?

Answer: System Information provides detailed information about hardware and software components. I use it for system profiling and troubleshooting.

3. Describe your experience using Apple Remote Desktop for remote system diagnostics and management.

Answer: Apple Remote Desktop allows for remote administration of Macs. I use it for troubleshooting, software distribution, and system management across multiple Macs.

4. How do you leverage iCloud Diagnostics for troubleshooting issues related to Apple ID and iCloud services?

Answer:iCloud Diagnostics provides information about iCloud services and Apple ID. I use it to troubleshoot issues related to syncing, account authentication, and iCloud features.

Security and Privacy Considerations:

1. Explain how you would use the logs to identify and address security-related incidents on a macOS system.

Answer:I review security-related logs for signs of unauthorized access, malware, or other security threats. Analyzing logs helps in detecting and mitigating security incidents.

2. Describe your experience using the Apple T2 Security Chip for enhanced security features and diagnostics.

Answer: The T2 chip provides secure boot, encrypted storage, and other security features. I use it to enhance system security and diagnostics.

3. How do you approach diagnosing privacy-related issues on a Mac, such as unauthorized access to sensitive information?

Answer:I review logs for unusual activities, enable FileVault for disk encryption, and regularly audit user permissions to prevent unauthorized access.

Troubleshooting Strategies:

1. Describe your approach to diagnosing and resolving intermittent issues that don't consistently appear.

Answer:I gather as much information as possible, use diagnostic tools to capture system state during the issue, and analyze logs to identify patterns or triggers.

2. How do you prioritize and address multiple concurrent issues affecting a macOS system?

Answer:I prioritize based on the impact on productivity and critical system functions. I address critical issues first and then move on to less urgent ones.

3. Explain your strategy for diagnosing issues reported by users that may not have a clear error message or symptom.

Answer:I engage with users to gather detailed information about their experiences, replicate issues where possible, and use diagnostic tools to uncover underlying causes.

Documentation and Reporting:

1. How do you document your diagnostic process and findings for future reference or for collaborating with other team members?

Answer:I maintain detailed documentation of diagnostic steps, findings, and solutions. This documentation helps in knowledge sharing and future reference.

2. Describe a situation where you had to create a detailed diagnostic report for management or other stakeholders.

Answer:I provide a detailed summary of the issue, steps taken for diagnosis, and recommendations for resolution. Clear and concise reports aid in decision-making.

Continuous Learning and Adaptability:

1. How do you stay updated on the latest diagnostic tools and techniques in the macOS environment?

Answer:I regularly attend Apple developer conferences, participate in online forums, and follow Apple's official documentation and updates to stay informed about new tools and techniques.

2. Describe a challenging diagnostic issue you faced recently and how you approached and resolved it.

Answer:I encountered a kernel panic issue that required a deep dive into kernel logs and crash reports. I identified a driver conflict, updated the driver, and resolved the issue.

Collaboration and Communication:

1. How do you communicate technical issues and solutions to non-technical stakeholders or end-users?

Answer:I translate technical details into clear and understandable language, focusing on the impact of the issue and steps taken for resolution.

2. Explain how you collaborate with other IT professionals or teams to address complex macOS issues.

Answer:I engage in open communication, share diagnostic findings, and collaborate on solutions. Regular team meetings and knowledge-sharing sessions contribute to a collective understanding of macOS issues and solutions.

Handling System Crashes

Understanding System Crashes:

1. What is a kernel panic, and how does it differ from a regular system crash?

Answer:A kernel panic is a specific type of system crash that occurs at the kernel level. It's more severe than a regular application crash and requires system reboot.

2. Can you explain the significance of a core dump in the context of a system crash on macOS?

Answer:A core dump is a file that captures the memory contents of a crashed process. It is valuable for post-mortem analysis to understand the state of the application at the time of the crash.

3. How would you differentiate between a hardware-related system crash and a software-related one on a Mac?

Answer: Hardware-related crashes often involve issues with components like RAM or storage. Software-related crashes are more likely due to bugs, incompatible drivers, or corrupt system files.

Diagnosing System Crashes:

1. Describe the steps you would take to analyze a kernel panic on a Mac.

Answer:I would start by reviewing panic logs using Console or analysing the panic report. This includes checking for specific error messages, timestamps, and potentially identifying the driver or process causing the panic.

2. How do you approach diagnosing a system crash when there is no clear error message or panic report?

Answer:I would use diagnostic tools like Console, Activity Monitor, and system logs to look for patterns or anomalies leading up to the crash. Identifying common factors can help narrow down the root cause.

3. Explain your experience with using the "sysdiagnose" command for collecting diagnostic information after a system crash.

Answer:sysdiagnose gathers a comprehensive set of diagnostic information. I use it to collect data, including logs, crash reports, and system state, immediately after a crash for in-depth analysis.

4. What role does the Console application play in diagnosing system crashes, and how do you utilize it effectively?

Answer: Console provides access to system logs, crash reports, and diagnostic messages. I use it to identify patterns, error messages, and events leading up to the crash.

Kernel Panics and Extensions:

1. How do you troubleshoot kernel panics caused by third-party kernel extensions?

Answer:I start by disabling or removing third-party kernel extensions. If the issue resolves, I gradually reintroduce them to identify the specific extension causing the kernel panic.

2. Explain the concept of kextcache and its relevance in diagnosing and resolving kernel extension-related issues.

Answer:kextcache is used to rebuild the kernel extension cache. If there are issues with extensions, rebuilding the cache can help resolve conflicts and ensure the system loads them correctly.

3. What steps would you take if a Mac experiences recurring kernel panics after a system update?

Answer:I would check for incompatible third-party software or kernel extensions, verify system integrity using Disk Utility, and potentially roll back the update if necessary.

Memory and Hardware Issues:

1. How do you diagnose system crashes related to faulty RAM on a Mac?

Answer:I use the built-in Memory Diagnostics tool, check memory usage using Activity Monitor, and perform hardware tests to identify and replace faulty RAM modules.

2. Can you explain how to use the Apple Hardware Test or Apple Diagnostics to identify and address hardware-related system crashes?

Answer: Apple Hardware Test (for older Macs) or Apple Diagnostics (for newer Macs) can perform hardware tests. I interpret the results to identify and address issues with components like RAM or storage.

3. What role does the SMART status of a hard drive play in diagnosing system crashes, and how do you check it?

Answer: The SMART status indicates the health of a hard drive. I use Disk Utility to check the SMART status, and if issues are detected, I replace or repair the drive.

Software-Related System Crashes:

1. How do you approach diagnosing system crashes caused by incompatible or outdated software on a Mac?

Answer:I check for software updates, review crash reports for specific applications, and systematically disable or uninstall third-party software to identify the culprit.

2. Explain your approach to troubleshooting system crashes related to macOS updates or patches.

Answer:I review system logs, check for known issues with the update, and verify the compatibility of third-party software. If necessary, I roll back the update until a resolution is available.

3. What steps would you take to diagnose and resolve a system crash caused by a corrupt user profile or preferences?

Answer:I create a new user account to check if the issue persists. If not, I transfer data to the new account. Otherwise, I reset user preferences and profile settings.

Performance Monitoring and Bottlenecks:

1. How do you use performance monitoring tools to identify potential bottlenecks leading to system crashes?

Answer:I use tools like Activity Monitor and top to monitor CPU, memory, disk, and network usage. Anomalies or spikes in these metrics can help identify potential performance bottlenecks.

2. Can you explain the significance of disk I/O and how it can contribute to system crashes?

Answer: Disk I/O issues, such as excessive read or write operations, can lead to performance degradation and system crashes. Monitoring disk activity using tools like iostat helps identify such issues.

3. Describe your experience using the "sudo fs_usage" command to monitor file system activity and diagnose system crashes.

Answer:fs_usage provides real-time file system activity. I use it to identify processes causing excessive file operations, helping to diagnose and resolve performance-related issues.

Network-Related System Crashes:

1. How do you approach diagnosing system crashes caused by network issues, such as excessive traffic or connectivity problems?

Answer:I use network diagnostic tools like netstat and Wireshark to monitor network activity, check for packet loss, and identify potential network-related issues leading to crashes.

2. Explain your experience using the "ping" and "traceroute" commands to diagnose and troubleshoot network-related system crashes.

Answer:I use "ping" to check connectivity and "traceroute" to identify network hops and latency issues. Analyzing the results helps diagnose and troubleshoot network problems.

Advanced System Crash Scenarios:

1. Describe a situation where you had to diagnose and address a recurring system crash that occurred intermittently.

Answer:I would share an experience where I systematically gathered data during each crash, analyzed logs, and used diagnostic tools to identify common factors leading to the intermittent crashes.

2. How do you handle a situation where a system crash occurs during critical operations, such as software development or server maintenance?

Answer:I prioritize data recovery and system stability. I might implement temporary workarounds, roll back recent changes, and conduct a post-mortem analysis to prevent future occurrences.

3. Explain your strategy for preventing data loss during a system crash and recovering critical files afterward.

Answer: Regular backups, including Time Machine or other backup solutions, are essential. In the event of a crash, I prioritize data recovery from backups to minimize data loss.

Collaboration and Communication:

1. How do you communicate with end-users or stakeholders during and after a system crash to manage expectations and provide updates?

Answer:I communicate transparently, providing timely updates on the investigation, potential resolutions, and steps being taken to prevent future occurrences.

2. Describe a scenario where you collaborated with other IT professionals or teams to address a complex system crash issue.

Answer:I would share an experience where cross-functional collaboration was essential, involving system administrators, developers, and possibly hardware specialists to collectively address the issue.

Documentation and Post-Mortem Analysis:

1. How do you document your diagnostic process and findings during a system crash investigation?

Answer:I maintain detailed documentation, including steps taken, diagnostic results, and resolutions. This documentation is crucial for future reference and knowledge sharing.

2. Explain your approach to conducting a post-mortem analysis after resolving a system crash to prevent future occurrences.

Answer:I conduct a thorough review of the incident, identify root causes, and propose preventive measures. This analysis contributes to improving system stability and preventing similar issues.

Continuous Learning and Adaptability:

1. How do you stay updated on the latest diagnostic tools and techniques for handling system crashes on macOS?

Answer:I regularly participate in training programs, attend conferences, and stay connected with online communities to stay informed about the latest tools and best practices.

2. Describe a situation where you had to adapt your diagnostic approach to a new or unfamiliar system crash scenario.

Answer:I would share an experience where I encountered a unique or unexpected system crash, and I had to adapt my diagnostic approach by exploring new tools or techniques to resolve the issue.

ONLINE RESOURCES

Practice Paper Link: https://forms.gle/HQApzNo314pBEiY6A

QR Code:

Video Link: https://www.youtube.com/playlist?list=PLzlh_31VWEFphKu-eJx1KnT18uETnLAGU

QR Code:

Chapter 11: mac OS Updates and Upgrades

mac OS Versioning and Naming

Understanding macOS Versioning:

1. Can you explain the typical structure of a macOS version number?

Answer:macOS version numbers follow a format like "X.Y.Z," where X is the major version, Y is the minor version, and Z is the patch or build number.

2. What is the significance of the major version number in macOS?

Answer: The major version represents significant updates, features, and changes to the operating system. Major updates are often accompanied by a change in the marketing name.

3. How does Apple typically name macOS versions, and what is the significance of using California-based names in recent releases?

Answer: Apple names macOS versions after locations in California. The names help create a consistent branding strategy, and each release reflects a theme or characteristic associated with the chosen location.

4. Explain the difference between a macOS "point" release (e.g., macOS 10.15 to macOS 10.15.1) and a major release (e.g., macOS 10.14 to macOS 10.15).

Answer: Point releases typically include bug fixes, security updates, and minor improvements. Major releases introduce significant new features, changes to the user interface, and improvements to the overall system.

History and Evolution:

1. Can you provide an overview of the transition from Mac OS 9 to macOS, including the significance of macOS X?

Answer:macOS X marked a shift from the classic Mac OS (Mac OS 9) to a Unix-based operating system. It introduced a new architecture, improved stability, and laid the foundation for future macOS versions.

2. Explain the significance of macOS versions like Leopard (10.5), Snow Leopard (10.6), and Mountain Lion (10.8) in terms of features and improvements.

Answer: Leopard introduced Time Machine and Spaces, Snow Leopard focused on performance and optimization, and Mountain Lion emphasized integration with iOS features like iCloud and Notification Center.

3. Discuss the transition from macOS X versions to macOS 11 Big Sur and the introduction of the M1 chip.

Answer:macOS 11 Big Sur marked a significant design overhaul, introducing a refreshed user interface. The transition to Apple Silicon with the M1 chip represented a shift in Mac architecture, enhancing performance and efficiency.

4. How has the macOS versioning strategy changed with the introduction of annual updates at WWDC?

Answer: Apple shifted to an annual release cycle announced at WWDC, providing a predictable schedule for developers and users. This approach allows for regular feature updates and improvements.

User Interface Changes:

1. Discuss the user interface changes introduced in macOS versions like Mojave (10.14) and Catalina (10.15).

Answer: Mojave introduced Dark Mode, dynamic desktop wallpapers, and a redesigned Mac App Store. Catalina featured the separation of iTunes into Music, Podcasts, and TV apps, along with iPad app support.

2. How has macOS Big Sur (11) impacted the user interface, and what are the key design elements introduced?

Answer: Big Sur brought a unified design with rounded corners, updated icons, and a Control Center. The menu bar and dock were redesigned to provide a cohesive and visually appealing experience.

Compatibility and System Requirements:

1. Discuss the considerations and challenges associated with upgrading older Mac hardware to the latest macOS version.

Answer: New macOS versions may have higher system requirements, including compatibility with specific processors or features. Older hardware may not support all the features of the latest macOS.

2. How do you manage compatibility issues when upgrading software applications during a macOS version transition?

Answer:I ensure that all essential applications are compatible with the new macOS version before upgrading. If compatibility issues arise, I collaborate with developers or explore alternative applications.

Security and Privacy Features:

1. Describe the security enhancements introduced in recent macOS versions and how they contribute to overall system protection.

Answer: Features like Gatekeeper, System Integrity Protection (SIP), and FileVault contribute to macOS security. Regular updates include patches for known vulnerabilities, enhancing the system's resistance to exploits.

2. How has Apple addressed user privacy concerns in macOS, and what features have been introduced to enhance user control over data?

Answer: Features like App Tracking Transparency and Privacy Nutrition Labels in the Mac App Store aim to provide users with more transparency and control over how their data is used.

Naming Conventions:

1. What is the significance of Apple's shift to using California landmarks in macOS names, such as El Capitan, Sierra, and Mojave?

Answer: The use of California landmarks adds a thematic and recognizable element to macOS version names, creating a consistent and memorable branding strategy.

2. Discuss the naming conventions of macOS versions before the shift to California landmarks. How were they named, and what was the inspiration?

Answer: Before California landmarks, macOS versions were named after big cats (e.g., Cheetah, Jaguar, Panther). This naming convention symbolized speed and agility.

Developer Tools and APIs:

1. How has Xcode evolved across macOS versions, and what developer tools have been introduced to enhance the development experience?

Answer: Xcode has evolved with each macOS version, introducing features like SwiftUI for declarative UI development, Metal for high-performance graphics, and updates to Swift, Apple's programming language.

2. Discuss the significance of the transition to Apple Silicon for developers and how it has influenced macOS application development.

Answer: The transition to Apple Silicon required developers to update their applications to be compatible with the new architecture. Apple provides tools like Rosetta 2 to ensure compatibility during the transition period.

System Integrity and Recovery:

1. Explain the role of System Integrity Protection (SIP) in macOS, and how it contributes to system stability and security.

Answer:SIP protects critical system files and directories from being modified, even by privileged users. It enhances system stability and prevents unauthorized changes.

2. How do you approach recovery and troubleshooting when a macOS system becomes unresponsive or encounters persistent issues after an upgrade?

Answer:I use macOS recovery tools like Disk Utility, Terminal, and reinstall options to troubleshoot issues. If necessary, I refer to system logs and diagnostic tools to identify the root cause.

Performance Optimization:

1. Describe your approach to optimizing system performance after a macOS upgrade to ensure a smooth user experience.

Answer:I monitor system performance using tools like Activity Monitor, address resource-intensive processes, and optimize settings for features introduced in the new macOS version.

2. How do you leverage the Performance pane in Activity Monitor to identify and address performance bottlenecks?

Answer: The Performance pane in Activity Monitor provides insights into CPU, memory, energy, and disk usage. I use it to identify resource-intensive processes and optimize system performance.

Upgrading to Newer mac OS Versions

Technical Questions:

1. Can you outline the typical steps involved in upgrading macOS to a newer version?

Answer: The process generally includes backing up data, checking system requirements, downloading the new OS, and performing the installation.

2. How do you handle compatibility issues with third-party applications during an OS upgrade?

Answer: I identify and update incompatible applications before the upgrade, ensuring they are compatible with the newer macOS version.

3. Explain the significance of creating a backup before upgrading macOS.

Answer: Creating a backup is crucial to safeguard data in case of any unforeseen issues during the upgrade. Time Machine or similar tools are commonly used for this purpose.

4. How do you troubleshoot a failed macOS upgrade?

Answer: I start by checking system logs for error messages, examining available disk space, and ensuring the hardware meets the new OS requirements. If needed, I perform a clean installation.

5. What considerations should be taken into account when upgrading macOS in an enterprise environment?

Answer: Enterprise upgrades require meticulous planning, including compatibility testing with business-critical applications, employee training, and communication strategies to minimize disruptions.

6. Describe how you handle firmware updates that might be required during a macOS upgrade.

Answer: I ensure that all firmware updates are applied before initiating the macOS upgrade to guarantee compatibility with the new operating system.

7. How do you manage the upgrade process in environments with a large number of Mac devices?

Answer: Centralized management tools like Jamf Pro are effective for deploying and managing macOS upgrades across a fleet of Mac devices, ensuring a streamlined and consistent process.

8. Can you explain the difference between an upgrade and a clean installation of macOS?

Answer: An upgrade installs the new OS while preserving user data and applications, while a clean installation involves erasing the existing system and starting fresh with the new OS.

9. What role does user training play in a successful macOS upgrade?

Answer: User training is essential to familiarize employees with new features and changes, reducing the likelihood of confusion and productivity disruptions after the upgrade.

10. How do you ensure data integrity during the upgrade process?

Answer: I verify the integrity of the backup before starting the upgrade, and I monitor the installation process to catch any errors that could compromise data integrity.

Soft Skills and Communication:

1. How do you communicate the benefits of upgrading to a newer macOS version to non-technical stakeholders?

Answer: I emphasize improved security, performance enhancements, and new features in a way that aligns with the organization's goals and objectives.

2. How do you prioritize and manage multiple macOS upgrade projects simultaneously?

Answer: I employ project management methodologies to prioritize tasks, allocate resources efficiently, and ensure timely completion of each upgrade project.

3. Describe a situation where you had to manage resistance from users during a macOS upgrade. How did you handle it?

Answer: I engaged with users early in the process, addressing concerns and providing clear communication about the benefits of the upgrade. User feedback was incorporated where possible.

4. How do you stay informed about the latest macOS updates, features, and security patches?

Answer: I regularly follow Apple's official channels, participate in forums, and subscribe to relevant newsletters and blogs to stay updated on the latest macOS developments.

5. Can you give an example of a time when an unexpected issue arose during a macOS upgrade, and how did you handle it?

Answer: I encountered a third-party driver compatibility issue that caused system instability. I rolled back the upgrade, identified the problematic driver, and worked with the vendor to resolve the issue before proceeding.

6. Explain how you ensure a smooth transition for end-users after a macOS upgrade.

Answer: I provide comprehensive training materials, host workshops, and offer post-upgrade support to address any questions or issues users may have during the transition period.

7. How do you balance the need for timely upgrades with the potential for disruptions to business operations?

Answer: I conduct thorough planning and scheduling to minimize disruptions, often performing upgrades during off-peak hours or in phases to ensure business continuity.

8. Describe your approach to managing and resolving conflicts that may arise between different software components after a macOS upgrade.

Answer: I systematically identify and address conflicts by collaborating with software vendors, applying patches, and, if necessary, seeking alternative solutions to ensure a harmonious system.

9. How do you handle situations where an upgrade is essential for security reasons, but critical applications are not yet compatible with the new macOS version?

Answer: I collaborate with application vendors to expedite compatibility updates, implement temporary security measures, and closely monitor the situation until a viable solution is in place.

10. How do you decide whether a macOS upgrade is suitable for a particular set of hardware, considering the organization's budget constraints?

Answer: I conduct a cost-benefit analysis, taking into account the security improvements, performance enhancements, and new features offered by the upgrade against the potential hardware upgrade costs.

Project Management and Planning:

1. What steps do you take to ensure that all necessary preparations are made before initiating a macOS upgrade?

Answer: I follow a detailed checklist that includes tasks such as data backup, application compatibility checks, user communication, and a rollback plan in case of unexpected issues.

2. How do you approach testing macOS upgrades in a staging environment before deploying them organization-wide?

Answer: I set up a representative test environment mirroring the production environment, perform thorough testing with various use cases, and involve key stakeholders to validate the results.

3. Explain the importance of creating a rollback plan and how you implement it during a macOS upgrade.

Answer: A rollback plan is crucial for mitigating risks. I create system backups, document each step of the upgrade process, and establish criteria for determining when a rollback is necessary.

4. How do you handle situations where a macOS upgrade is delayed due to unforeseen circumstances?

Answer: I communicate transparently with stakeholders, provide regular updates, and adjust project timelines as needed. Flexibility and adaptability are key in such situations.

5. Describe your approach to post-upgrade monitoring and support.

Answer: I implement monitoring tools to identify any post-upgrade issues promptly. I also establish a support system to address user inquiries and issues, ensuring a smooth post-upgrade experience.

6. Can you share an experience where a macOS upgrade project was completed ahead of schedule? What contributed to its success?

Answer: Early planning, efficient resource allocation, and a proactive approach to issue resolution contributed to completing a macOS upgrade project ahead of schedule.

7. How do you determine the appropriate time to schedule a macOS upgrade to minimize disruptions to end-users?

Answer: I analyze usage patterns, consult with key stakeholders, and schedule upgrades during periods of low user activity to minimize disruptions and downtime.

8. In what ways do you ensure that all necessary documentation is in place for a macOS upgrade project?

Answer: I maintain detailed documentation for each phase of the project, including system configurations, upgrade steps, user communication plans, and post-upgrade support procedures.

9. How do you handle dependencies on third-party services that may be impacted by a macOS upgrade?

Answer: I collaborate with service providers, confirm compatibility, and schedule upgrades to align with their maintenance windows to minimize any potential service disruptions.

10. How do you ensure that the organization remains compliant with regulatory requirements during and after a macOS upgrade?

Answer: I collaborate with legal and compliance teams to understand and address regulatory requirements, ensuring that the macOS upgrade does not compromise data security or regulatory compliance.

Security and Data Protection:

1. How do you ensure that sensitive data is protected during a macOS upgrade?

Answer: I use encryption for backups, implement secure update channels, and closely monitor the upgrade process to detect and address any potential security vulnerabilities.

2. Explain the role of system hardening in the context of a macOS upgrade.

Answer: System hardening involves securing the operating system by disabling unnecessary services, configuring firewalls, and implementing security best practices to enhance overall system security.

3. How do you address security concerns related to third-party software that may not receive immediate updates for a new macOS version?

Answer: I assess the risk, implement temporary mitigations if necessary, and closely monitor vendor communications for updates. Communication with users about potential risks is also a key component.

4. Describe your approach to handling security patches and updates after a macOS upgrade.

Answer: I stay vigilant for security patches released by Apple and third-party vendors, promptly applying them to maintain the integrity and security of the upgraded macOS environment.

5. In what ways do you ensure that the organization's security policies are consistently enforced after a macOS upgrade?

Answer: I conduct regular security audits, implement configuration management tools, and provide ongoing security training to ensure that security policies are understood and followed by all users.

Emerging Technologies and Trends:

1. How do you incorporate the latest advancements in Apple technologies into your macOS upgrade strategy?

Answer: I stay informed about Apple's roadmap, evaluate new features, and assess their relevance to the organization's goals. I then incorporate relevant advancements into the upgrade strategy.

2. Describe your experience with managing macOS upgrades in a hybrid environment that includes both Mac and non-Mac systems.

Answer: I develop cross-platform compatibility strategies, ensuring that Mac systems seamlessly integrate with non-Mac systems and that all users experience a consistent and secure computing environment.

3. How do you handle macOS upgrades in environments with a Bring Your Own Device (BYOD) policy?

Answer: I establish clear guidelines for users, ensuring that their devices meet the necessary requirements for the upgrade. I also provide support for users who may encounter issues during the upgrade process.

4. Can you discuss your experience with managing macOS upgrades in virtualized environments?

Answer: I leverage virtualization technologies to create test environments that mimic the production environment, allowing for comprehensive testing of macOS upgrades before deployment.

5. How do you stay ahead of emerging cybersecurity threats that may impact macOS upgrades?

Answer: I actively participate in cybersecurity communities, attend relevant conferences, and continuously update my knowledge on emerging threats to proactively incorporate security measures into macOS upgrade strategies.

Compatibility Considerations

Technical Questions:

1. How do you assess the compatibility of existing applications with a new macOS version?

Answer: I review application vendor documentation, check for updates, and test applications in a controlled environment to identify and address compatibility issues.

2. Can you explain the significance of kernel extensions in macOS compatibility?

Answer: Kernel extensions are crucial for hardware and software interactions. I ensure they are updated and compatible with the new macOS version to prevent system instability.

3. How do you handle situations where legacy hardware lacks drivers for a newer macOS version?

Answer: I explore alternative driver sources, work with third-party developers, and, if necessary, advise on upgrading hardware to maintain compatibility.

4. Describe your approach to testing peripheral device compatibility after a macOS upgrade.

Answer: I create a comprehensive testing plan that includes printers, scanners, and other peripherals, ensuring they function seamlessly with the upgraded macOS.

5. How do you address compatibility challenges when dealing with 32-bit applications in a macOS upgrade?

Answer: I identify 32-bit applications, communicate with vendors for updates, and explore virtualization or alternative solutions for critical applications without 64-bit support.

6. Can you discuss your experience with managing compatibility in mixed macOS and Windows environments?

Answer: I implement cross-platform solutions, such as virtualization or compatibility layers, to ensure smooth interactions between macOS and Windows systems.

7. How do you handle compatibility issues related to custom in-house applications during a macOS upgrade?

Answer: I collaborate with developers to update or modify the applications, conduct extensive testing, and implement fallback plans to minimize disruptions.

8.Explain the role of API changes in macOS upgrades and how they impact application compatibility.

Answer: API changes can break existing functionality. I closely monitor Apple's documentation, update code accordingly, and work with developers to ensure smooth transitions.

9. How do you prioritize application compatibility testing for a large software portfolio during a macOS upgrade?

Answer: I categorize applications based on criticality, user dependencies, and business impact, focusing on high-priority applications first to minimize potential disruptions.

10. Describe your experience with managing compatibility for macOS in enterprise environments with custom configurations.

Answer: I create standardized configurations, closely monitor changes, and collaborate with system administrators to ensure that custom configurations remain compatible after macOS upgrades.

Soft Skills and Communication:

1. How do you communicate compatibility requirements and potential issues to non-technical stakeholders during a macOS upgrade project?

Answer: I use clear, non-technical language to explain the importance of compatibility, potential impacts, and the steps being taken to ensure a smooth transition.

2. Can you share an experience where effective communication mitigated concerns related to compatibility during a macOS upgrade?

Answer: I held regular briefings, addressed concerns proactively, and provided a platform for users to ask questions, easing anxieties and ensuring a positive upgrade experience.

3. How do you collaborate with software vendors to address compatibility issues during a macOS upgrade?

Answer: I establish communication channels, participate in beta programs, and work closely with vendors to ensure timely updates and resolutions to compatibility issues.

4. Describe a situation where you had to manage conflicting requirements between user demands for new features and the need for compatibility in a macOS upgrade.

Answer: I prioritize compatibility to ensure system stability, while also engaging users in discussions about the benefits of the new features and potential workarounds for critical applications.

5. How do you approach providing user training on changes resulting from compatibility considerations in a macOS upgrade?

Answer: I create user-friendly training materials, conduct workshops, and offer support channels to help users adapt to changes and understand the reasons behind compatibility decisions.

6. Explain how you handle situations where business units have specific software requirements that may pose compatibility challenges in a macOS upgrade.

Answer: I collaborate with business units to understand their requirements, explore alternative solutions, and find compromises that maintain overall system compatibility.

7. How do you address concerns related to downtime and disruptions caused by compatibility issues during a macOS upgrade?

Answer: I schedule upgrades during off-peak hours, communicate downtime expectations clearly, and implement rollback plans to minimize disruptions in case of unexpected issues.

8. Describe your approach to managing user expectations regarding application availability and performance after a macOS upgrade.

Answer: I set realistic expectations, communicate potential challenges, and provide regular updates to keep users informed about the progress of the upgrade and any impact on applications.

9. How do you handle situations where users are resistant to changes resulting from compatibility considerations in a macOS upgrade?

Answer: I engage with users early in the process, gather feedback, and address concerns transparently. I highlight the benefits of the upgrade and offer support during the transition.

10. Can you discuss your experience with facilitating communication between different teams, such as IT, developers, and end-users, to ensure compatibility in macOS upgrades?

Answer: I establish regular communication channels, conduct cross-functional meetings, and create a collaborative environment to address compatibility challenges and share insights.

Project Management and Planning:

1. How do you prioritize compatibility testing for a macOS upgrade when dealing with limited resources and tight timelines?

Answer: I conduct risk assessments, focus on critical applications first, and use automation where possible to optimize testing processes and meet tight deadlines.

2. Describe your approach to creating a comprehensive compatibility testing plan for a macOS upgrade.

Answer: I identify critical applications, document compatibility requirements, establish testing environments, and define testing criteria to ensure thorough coverage.

3. How do you manage compatibility considerations when dealing with phased rollouts of a macOS upgrade in a large organization?

Answer: I prioritize departments based on critical functions, conduct phased rollouts, and closely monitor each phase to identify and address compatibility issues promptly.

4. Explain the importance of conducting a pilot phase in the context of macOS upgrades and compatibility testing.

Answer: A pilot phase allows for real-world testing with a smaller group, providing valuable feedback and identifying potential compatibility issues before a broader rollout.

5. How do you handle situations where compatibility issues arise post-deployment of a macOS upgrade?

Answer: I have post-deployment monitoring systems in place, a responsive support team, and a rollback plan if needed to quickly address and rectify compatibility issues.

6. Can you share an experience where meticulous planning and execution led to a successful macOS upgrade with minimal compatibility issues?

Answer: Detailed testing, proactive communication, and a well-defined rollback plan contributed to a successful macOS upgrade with minimal disruptions and compatibility issues.

7. How do you coordinate with IT support teams to ensure they are adequately prepared to handle compatibility-related inquiries and issues after a macOS upgrade?

Answer: I provide comprehensive training materials, conduct workshops, and establish dedicated support channels to ensure IT support teams are well-equipped to address compatibility issues.

8. In what ways do you ensure that compatibility considerations are integrated into the overall project timeline for a macOS upgrade?

Answer: I collaborate with project managers to ensure compatibility tasks are integrated into the project timeline, with clear milestones and dependencies identified.

9. How do you balance the need for a timely macOS upgrade with the thoroughness required for compatibility testing?

Answer: I employ risk-based testing, prioritizing critical applications, and using automated testing where applicable to strike a balance between speed and thoroughness.

10. How do you ensure that all stakeholders are involved in the decision-making process regarding compatibility considerations in a macOS upgrade?

Answer: I organize regular meetings with key stakeholders, gather input, and ensure that decisions related to compatibility align with the organization's overall goals.

Security and Data Protection:

1. Explain how you ensure that compatibility considerations do not compromise the security of a macOS system during an upgrade.

Answer: I closely monitor security updates, assess third-party software for vulnerabilities, and prioritize security patches to maintain a balance between compatibility and system security.

2. How do you handle situations where security updates are required for applications to maintain compatibility with a new macOS version?

Answer: I collaborate with application vendors to expedite security updates, implement temporary security measures if necessary, and communicate transparently with users about the situation.

3. Describe your experience with managing compatibility considerations in environments with strict regulatory requirements.

Answer: I collaborate with compliance teams, conduct thorough assessments, and ensure that compatibility decisions align with regulatory requirements to maintain data integrity and security.

4. Can you discuss your approach to balancing the need for frequent security updates with the stability requirements of critical applications in a macOS environment?

Answer: I establish a risk-based approach, prioritizing critical security updates and closely monitoring the impact on critical applications to strike a balance between security and stability.

5. How do you address potential security vulnerabilities related to outdated software versions that may be present due to compatibility requirements?

Answer: I assess the risk, communicate with stakeholders, and work to expedite updates or replacements for outdated software to maintain a secure computing environment.

Emerging Technologies and Trends:

1. How do you stay informed about the latest advancements in macOS technologies and their impact on compatibility considerations?

Answer: I regularly follow Apple's developer documentation, participate in beta programs, and engage with the developer community to stay ahead of emerging macOS technologies.

2. Describe your experience with managing compatibility considerations in macOS environments using Apple Silicon processors.

Answer: I adapt testing procedures to include compatibility with Apple Silicon, collaborate with developers for architecture-specific updates, and ensure a smooth transition for users.

3. In what ways do you incorporate advancements in cloud computing into your strategy for managing compatibility in macOS environments?

Answer: I assess the impact of cloud services on application compatibility, evaluate cloud-based solutions, and ensure seamless integration with macOS environments.

4. How do you handle compatibility considerations in environments using virtualization technologies for macOS systems?

Answer: I implement virtualization-aware testing procedures, collaborate with virtualization solution providers, and ensure compatibility with macOS upgrades in virtualized environments.

5. Can you discuss your approach to managing compatibility considerations in a macOS environment that includes Internet of Things (IoT) devices?

Answer: I evaluate the compatibility of IoT devices with new macOS versions, work with device manufacturers to address compatibility issues, and ensure a secure and integrated environment.

ONLINE RESOURCES

Practice Paper Link: https://forms.gle/ZeBEktoy5CxXA1pt8

QR Code:

Video Link: https://www.youtube.com/playlist?list=PLzlh_31VWEFo3cdjLQMQZUDtoK8RUlvkS

QR Code:

Chapter 12: mac OS System Administration

User and Group Management

Technical Questions:

1. Explain the difference between local and network user accounts on macOS.

Answer: Local user accounts are stored on a specific Mac, while network user accounts are stored on a server and can be accessed from multiple Macs.

2. How do you create a new user account in macOS, and what information is typically required?

Answer: I use the System Preferences or dscl command to create a new user, providing details such as username, full name, password, and account type.

3. Can you describe the purpose of the root user in macOS, and how do you enable or disable it?

Answer: The root user has superuser privileges. It's disabled by default, but I can enable it through the Directory Utility or by using the dsenableroot command.

4. Explain how you manage user account permissions and access rights in macOS.

Answer: I use the macOS permission system, adjusting settings with the chmod command or the Get Info dialog. Additionally, I leverage Access Control Lists (ACLs) for more granular control.

5. How do you configure macOS to allow or deny specific users or groups access to certain applications or system resources?

Answer: I use the built-in parental controls in System Preferences or leverage third-party tools to manage application and resource access for users or groups.

6. Describe the steps involved in resetting a user's password in macOS.

Answer: I can reset a user password through the Users & Groups section in System Preferences or by using the dscl command in Terminal.

7. How do you manage user account attributes, such as the home directory or login shell, in macOS?

Answer: I use the dscl command or Directory Utility to modify user attributes, adjusting settings like home directory path or login shell.

8. Can you explain the purpose of User Template folders in macOS, and how are they used in user account creation?

Answer: User Template folders contain default settings for new user accounts. They are replicated when creating a new user, providing a standardized initial environment.

9. How do you manage user authentication methods in macOS, including password policies and multi-factor authentication?

Answer: I configure password policies through the Password Policy settings in Directory Utility and enable multi-factor authentication options for increased security.

10. Explain the role of the macOS Keychain in user account management and security.

Answer: The Keychain stores passwords and other sensitive information securely. It's crucial for managing credentials and ensuring secure access to various services.

Soft Skills and Communication:

1. How do you communicate user account management procedures and policies to end-users in a clear and understandable way?

Answer: I create user-friendly documentation, conduct training sessions, and provide ongoing support to ensure users understand account management procedures and policies.

2. Describe a situation where you had to assist non-technical users in managing their accounts on macOS. How did you approach it?

Answer: I provided step-by-step guidance, offered training materials, and patiently assisted users in managing their accounts, ensuring they felt comfortable and empowered.

3. How do you handle user requests for elevated privileges or exceptions to standard user policies in macOS?

Answer: I evaluate the request's necessity, consult with relevant stakeholders, and, if appropriate, adjust privileges or policies while considering security implications.

4. Can you share an experience where effective communication prevented user confusion during a major user account management change?

Answer: I communicated changes in advance, explained the reasons behind them, and provided support channels, minimizing confusion and ensuring a smooth transition.

5. How do you collaborate with other IT teams to align user account management with broader IT strategies and security policies?

Answer: I participate in cross-functional meetings, share insights on user account management requirements, and collaborate on implementing policies that align with broader IT goals.

6. Explain how you would handle a situation where a user experiences difficulty accessing their account due to a configuration issue.

Answer: I would troubleshoot the issue, communicate transparently with the user, and provide clear instructions or assistance to resolve the problem promptly.

7. How do you prioritize and manage user account management tasks when dealing with a large user base?

Answer: I use automation for routine tasks, prioritize based on urgency and impact, and leverage tools like Apple Remote Desktop for efficient user account management at scale.

8. Describe your approach to providing user training on macOS security best practices, including password management and account protection.

Answer: I create engaging training materials, conduct workshops, and emphasize the importance of strong passwords, two-factor authentication, and other security best practices.

9. How do you handle situations where user account management changes are necessary due to compliance requirements?

Answer: I work closely with compliance teams, ensure user account management aligns with regulatory requirements, and communicate changes transparently to affected users.

10. Can you discuss your experience with managing user accounts in environments with diverse user roles and access requirements?

Answer: I customize user roles based on job responsibilities, implement role-based access controls, and regularly review and update user access to align with evolving needs.

Project Management and Planning:

1. How do you ensure that user account management practices align with industry best practices and Apple's recommended guidelines?

Answer: I regularly review Apple's documentation, participate in training programs, and stay informed about industry best practices to ensure user account management aligns with the latest standards.

2. Describe your approach to managing user account management tasks during system upgrades or maintenance windows.

Answer: I schedule user account management tasks during off-peak hours, communicate with users about potential disruptions, and use automation to streamline tasks during maintenance windows.

3. In what ways do you ensure that user account management tasks are securely executed, especially when handling sensitive information?

Answer: I implement secure protocols, use encrypted channels for communication, and adhere to security best practices to safeguard sensitive information during user account management tasks.

4. How do you approach delegating user account management responsibilities to other IT personnel while maintaining security and accountability?

Answer: I define clear roles and responsibilities, provide training to delegated personnel, and implement access controls to ensure accountability and maintain security standards.

5. Can you discuss your experience with managing user account management tasks in environments with a high level of user mobility, such as remote work scenarios?

Answer: I leverage mobile device management (MDM) solutions, implement secure remote access protocols, and conduct user training to ensure effective user account management in remote work scenarios.

6. How do you plan and execute the migration of user accounts from one macOS system to another while minimizing disruptions?

Answer: I conduct thorough planning, create migration checklists, use tools like Migration Assistant, and communicate with users to ensure a smooth transition.

7. Describe your approach to managing user account migrations when transitioning to a new macOS version or hardware platform.

Answer: I conduct compatibility assessments, create migration plans, and use tools like Time Machine or Apple's Migration Assistant to ensure a seamless transition to new macOS versions or hardware.

8. How do you manage user account provisioning and de-provisioning in macOS to align with employee onboarding and offboarding processes?

Answer: I collaborate with HR and IT teams, automate provisioning and de-provisioning processes, and conduct regular audits to ensure compliance with employee lifecycle changes.

9. Explain how you handle situations where user accounts need to be merged or split due to organizational changes.

Answer: I assess the requirements, plan the account modifications, and use appropriate tools and scripts to merge or split user accounts while preserving data integrity.

10. Can you share an experience where meticulous planning and execution led to a successful large-scale user account management project?

Answer: Detailed planning, stakeholder collaboration, and proactive communication contributed to the successful execution of a large-scale user account management project with minimal disruptions.

Security and Data Protection:

1. How do you ensure that user accounts are protected against unauthorized access or brute-force attacks in macOS?

Answer: I implement strong password policies, enable multi-factor authentication, and monitor authentication logs for suspicious activity to enhance user account security.

2. Describe your approach to managing user access and permissions to sensitive data to ensure data protection in macOS.

Answer: I apply the principle of least privilege, regularly review access controls, and use encryption for sensitive data to ensure comprehensive data protection in macOS.

3. How do you handle situations where users forget their passwords, and what measures do you have in place for secure password recovery?

Answer: I provide self-service password recovery options, such as security questions or email verification, while adhering to security protocols to prevent unauthorized access.

4. Explain how you manage user account security in macOS environments with a Bring Your Own Device (BYOD) policy.

Answer: I implement containerization solutions, enforce strong security policies, and provide guidance **on secure device configuration to maintain user account security in BYOD scenarios.**

5. In what ways do you ensure that user account management practices align with data privacy regulations, such as GDPR, in macOS environments?

Answer: I collaborate with legal and compliance teams, conduct privacy impact assessments, and implement user account management practices that align with the requirements of data privacy regulations.

Emerging Technologies and Trends:

1. How do you adapt user account management practices to incorporate new Apple technologies, such as Apple Silicon, into macOS environments?

Answer: I evaluate compatibility, work with developers for architecture-specific updates, and ensure seamless integration of user account management practices with new Apple technologies.

2. Can you discuss your experience with managing user accounts in macOS environments that utilize cloud-based identity and access management solutions?

Answer: I integrate cloud-based solutions with macOS user account management, ensuring secure authentication and access control while leveraging the benefits of cloud identity services.

3. In what ways do you incorporate advancements in artificial intelligence or machine learning into user account management strategies in macOS environments?

Answer: I explore AI-driven authentication methods, anomaly detection for user behavior, and machine learning for predicting access needs, ensuring a proactive and adaptive approach to user account management.

4. How do you address user account management challenges in macOS environments that include Internet of Things (IoT) devices?

Answer: I assess the compatibility of IoT devices with user accounts, work with device manufacturers to address user account management challenges, and ensure a secure and integrated environment.

5. Explain your approach to managing user accounts in macOS environments that involve virtualization technologies.

Answer: I leverage virtualization-aware user account management practices, ensuring compatibility and security in virtualized environments, and regularly testing user account functionality within virtual machines.

Disk Management and Optimization

Disk Management:

1. Explain the significance of APFS (Apple File System) in disk management.

Answer: APFS is Apple's modern file system designed for macOS. It supports features like snapshots, cloning, and native encryption, contributing to enhanced disk management capabilities.

2. How do you troubleshoot disk-related issues in macOS?

Answer: I use utilities like Disk Utility, Terminal commands (e.g., fsck), and system logs to identify and resolve disk-related problems.

3. What is Fusion Drive, and how does it optimize storage performance?

Answer: Fusion Drive combines SSD and HDD to create a single logical volume. macOS automatically manages data placement, promoting frequently accessed data to the faster SSD for improved performance.

4. How would you handle a situation where a disk is running out of space on a macOS system?

Answer: I would identify and remove unnecessary files, transfer data to an external drive, and potentially resize partitions using Disk Utility to reallocate space as needed.

5. Can you explain the role of Time Machine in disk management and backup on macOS?

Answer: Time Machine is a backup solution in macOS. It regularly backs up the entire system, providing a snapshot of the disk at various points in time, facilitating easy recovery in case of data loss.

6. Can you explain the process of disk initialization on macOS?

Answer: Disk initialization involves preparing a disk for use. In macOS, it typically involves using Disk Utility to format the disk with a compatible file system like APFS or HFS+.

7. How do you handle disk partitioning in macOS?

Answer: Disk Utility is the go-to tool for partitioning on macOS. It allows users to create, resize, and delete partitions, facilitating effective disk space management.

8. What is Core Storage, and how does it impact disk management in macOS?

Answer: Core Storage is a logical volume manager. It provides a layer of abstraction between the operating system and physical disks, enabling features like FileVault encryption and Fusion Drive.

Disk Optimization:

1. How can you monitor disk usage and performance in real-time on macOS?

Answer: Utilities like Activity Monitor provide real-time information on disk usage, I/O operations, and other performance metrics.

2. What strategies do you employ to prevent disk fragmentation on a Mac?

Answer: Regularly optimizing the file system with tools like Disk Utility, avoiding near-full disk conditions, and using APFS (which handles fragmentation efficiently) are effective strategies.

3. How would you optimize a Mac's startup time by managing startup items?

Answer: I would use the "Login Items" feature in System Preferences to control which applications launch at startup, ensuring only essential ones are enabled.

4. Can you discuss the role of Spotlight in disk optimization and how to manage its indexing?

Answer: Spotlight indexes files for quick searching. Managing Spotlight preferences in System Preferences allows you to exclude certain folders and optimize indexing for better performance.

5. How do you handle disk encryption in macOS, and what impact does it have on performance?

Answer: I use FileVault for disk encryption. While encryption may have a slight impact on performance, modern Macs with hardware encryption support typically minimize this effect.

6. How do you optimize disk performance on a Mac?

Answer: I optimize disk performance by regularly defragmenting files, managing startup items, and ensuring there is sufficient free space on the disk.

7. Explain the concept of TRIM support for SSDs in macOS.

Answer: TRIM is a feature that helps maintain the performance of SSDs by informing the drive which data blocks are no longer in use. macOS automatically supports TRIM for compatible SSDs.

General macOS and System Integration:

1. How does Disk Management tie into macOS system reliability and stability?

Answer: Effective disk management ensures data integrity, system stability, and contributes to a reliable computing environment.

2. Can you explain the concept of Time Machine snapshots and their impact on disk usage?

Answer: Time Machine snapshots capture the state of the file system at a specific point. While they consume disk space, macOS automatically manages and deletes older snapshots as needed.

3. How would you handle a situation where a disk suddenly becomes unresponsive or fails to mount on macOS?

Answer: I would first check Disk Utility for disk health and attempt to repair any issues. If necessary, I might use command-line tools like diskutil or explore hardware diagnostics.

4. Discuss the role of APFS in supporting features like snapshots and cloning in disk management.

Answer: APFS provides a foundation for features like snapshots and cloning, enabling users to create point-in-time copies of the file system and efficiently duplicate data.

5. How do you ensure data integrity and reliability when performing disk-related tasks on macOS?

Answer: I follow best practices, regularly back up data using Time Machine, verify disk health with Disk Utility, and monitor system logs for any signs of disk-related issues.

Advanced Disk Management:

1. Explain the process of converting a traditional hard drive to an APFS volume on macOS.

Answer: This involves using Disk Utility to create a new APFS volume and then migrating data from the old volume to the new one, ensuring compatibility and preserving data integrity.

2. How do you handle disk quotas and permissions on macOS in a multi-user environment?

Answer: Disk quotas can be managed using macOS Server or third-party solutions. Permissions are controlled through the file system, and I ensure proper user access using the chmod and chown commands.

3. Discuss the advantages and challenges of using RAID configurations for disk management on a Mac.

Answer: RAID configurations can improve performance and provide redundancy. However, they require careful setup, monitoring, and may have increased complexity in maintenance.

4. How can you optimize storage on a Mac with multiple drives, such as an external SSD and an internal HDD?

Answer: I would use the internal HDD for storage and the external SSD for frequently accessed files or applications, effectively leveraging the strengths of each drive.

5. Can you elaborate on the process of migrating data from an old Mac to a new one, including considerations for disk management?

Answer: I would use Migration Assistant to transfer data, ensuring both Macs are running compatible versions of macOS and have sufficient disk space for the migration.

Troubleshooting and Problem Resolution:

1. What steps would you take to address a situation where a Mac is experiencing slow read/write speeds on its disk?

Answer: I would first check for background processes affecting performance, run disk diagnostics, and consider upgrading to a faster disk if necessary.

2. How do you identify and resolve disk-related bottlenecks in a macOS system?

Answer: Performance monitoring tools like Activity Monitor and command-line utilities such as iostat help identify bottlenecks. I would then optimize or upgrade hardware accordingly.

3. Discuss the role of S.M.A.R.T. technology in predicting and preventing disk failures.

Answer: S.M.A.R.T. (Self-Monitoring, Analysis and Reporting Technology) provides real-time monitoring of disk health. I regularly check S.M.A.R.T. data to anticipate and address potential disk failures proactively.

4. How would you recover data from a corrupted disk or filesystem on macOS?

Answer: I would use Disk Utility for minor issues. For more severe cases, I might turn to data recovery software or services, ensuring that I follow proper procedures to avoid further data loss.

5. Can you provide an example of a challenging disk-related issue you've encountered and how you resolved it?

Answer: [Personalized response based on the candidate's experience.]

Integration with Other macOS Features:

1. How does iCloud integration impact disk management on a Mac?

Answer: iCloud Drive allows seamless storage of documents and data in the cloud, potentially reducing the local disk space required for certain files.

2. Explain how Full Disk Access and System Integrity Protection (SIP) influence disk-related tasks in macOS.

Answer: Full Disk Access allows certain apps to access protected areas of the disk, while SIP protects critical system files. Understanding these features is crucial for secure disk management.

3. How do you manage Time Machine backups when dealing with multiple disks on a Mac?

Answer: I configure Time Machine to include all relevant disks and ensure that backup destinations have sufficient space. Regularly monitoring backups is essential for data recovery.

4. Discuss the impact of macOS updates on disk management, and how do you prepare for these updates?

Answer: macOS updates may involve changes to file systems or disk structures. I ensure backups are current and verify software compatibility before initiating updates.

5. How can you leverage Terminal commands for advanced disk management tasks on macOS?

Answer: Terminal commands like diskutil and fsck provide powerful options for disk management. I use them for tasks such as repairing disks, managing partitions, and checking file system integrity.

Future Trends and Technologies:

1. How do you foresee emerging technologies, such as non-volatile memory and storage-class memory, influencing disk management on macOS in the coming years?

Answer: Emerging technologies may provide faster and more durable storage options. Adapting to these technologies will involve understanding their integration into the macOS ecosystem.

2. What role do you think machine learning and artificial intelligence might play in optimizing disk management processes on macOS?

Answer: Machine learning could enhance predictive analysis of disk usage patterns, helping users optimize storage and performance based on their specific usage habits.

3. How would you approach implementing a sustainable disk management strategy in an environment with a high volume of data and frequent changes?

Answer: I would focus on automation, regularly analyze usage patterns, and implement scalable solutions such as storage tiering to ensure efficient and sustainable disk management.

4. As storage technologies evolve, how would you adapt disk management strategies to accommodate new storage mediums and formats?

Answer: Staying informed about new storage technologies and their compatibility with macOS is crucial. Adapting disk management strategies involves integrating support for these new mediums and formats.

5. In a scenario where a Mac is used for resource-intensive tasks like video editing, how would you optimize disk performance to meet the demands of these tasks?

Answer: I would consider using high-performance SSDs, optimizing file systems, and implementing RAID configurations if necessary. Regular monitoring and adjustments based on the specific workflow would be essential.

Backup and Restore Strategies

Backup Strategies:

1. What are the key components of a comprehensive backup strategy for macOS?

Answer: A comprehensive backup strategy includes regular backups, multiple backup locations, versioning, and a combination of on-site and off-site backups for redundancy.

2. How do you prioritize data for backup, and what criteria do you consider when deciding on backup frequency?

Answer: I prioritize data based on its importance and criticality. Critical data may be backed up more frequently, and the frequency is determined by factors like data volatility and business needs.

3. Can you explain the difference between incremental and full backups, and when would you use each in a backup strategy?

Answer: Incremental backups only include changes since the last backup, conserving storage space and time. Full backups include all data. I use incremental backups for efficiency and full backups for comprehensive protection.

4. How do you handle large datasets in backup strategies, ensuring efficient use of storage while maintaining quick restore times?

Answer: I implement strategies like differential backups or use backup solutions with deduplication and compression features to optimize storage efficiency while maintaining quick restores.

5. Discuss the role of Time Machine in a macOS backup strategy.

Answer: Time Machine provides automated, incremental backups and allows users to restore their system to a specific point in time. It's an integral part of a macOS backup strategy.

6. What considerations do you take into account when selecting backup storage media (external drives, network-attached storage, cloud storage, etc.) for a macOS environment?

Answer: I consider factors like capacity, speed, security, and accessibility. The choice depends on the specific needs of the organization, balancing cost and performance.

7. How do you handle backing up macOS systems with multiple users and individualized data sets?

Answer: I ensure that each user's data is included in the backup, using features like Time Machine's support for multiple user accounts. File permissions are also considered to maintain data integrity.

8. Can you explain the importance of verifying backups and how you incorporate this into your backup strategy?

Answer: Verifying backups ensures data integrity. I regularly perform test restores and verify checksums to confirm that the backed-up data is consistent and can be successfully restored.

Restore Strategies:

1. Describe the steps you would take to restore a macOS system using Time Machine.

Answer: To restore a macOS system using Time Machine, I would boot into macOS Recovery, open Time Machine, select the desired backup, and follow the prompts to restore the system.

2. In the event of data loss, how do you prioritize data for restoration, and what factors influence your decision-making process?

Answer: I prioritize data based on criticality and importance to the user or organization. Business-critical data or data needed for immediate operations takes precedence.

3. Discuss the challenges and considerations when restoring data to a different macOS system with varying hardware configurations.

Answer: Challenges may include driver compatibility and hardware differences. I ensure compatibility and may need to reinstall certain drivers or applications to achieve a successful restore.

4. How do you address the potential issue of file versioning and conflicts during the restoration process?

Answer: I carefully manage file versioning, keeping track of changes. I may leverage backup solutions that support versioning and conflict resolution or manually address conflicts during the restore.

5. Explain the role of bootable backups in macOS restore strategies.

Answer: Bootable backups allow for quick system recovery by providing a fully functional system on an external drive. In case of a primary drive failure, users can boot directly from the backup.

6. How do you ensure data consistency and integrity during the restore process, especially when dealing with large datasets?

Answer: I use backup solutions that provide data verification features. Regularly testing restores, validating checksums, and monitoring for any errors are essential steps in ensuring data integrity.

7. Can you discuss the considerations and steps involved in restoring data from a cloud-based backup solution on macOS?

Answer: Restoring data from a cloud-based backup involves accessing the backup service, selecting the desired files or system state, and initiating the restore process while ensuring a stable internet connection.

Security and Compliance:

1. How do you ensure the security of backup data, particularly when using cloud-based backup solutions?

Answer: I implement encryption for backup data, both in transit and at rest. This ensures that even if the backup is stored in the cloud, it remains secure and compliant with data protection standards.

2. In a scenario where a macOS system is subject to industry-specific regulations (e.g., healthcare or finance), how do you design a backup strategy to comply with those regulations?

Answer: I align the backup strategy with regulatory requirements, ensuring data retention periods, encryption standards, and auditing capabilities are in place to meet compliance needs.

3. What measures do you take to protect backup infrastructure and prevent unauthorized access to backup data?

Answer: I implement access controls, encryption, and regular security audits. Secure physical and network access to backup infrastructure is crucial to prevent unauthorized tampering or data breaches.

4. Can you discuss the role of encryption in macOS backup strategies, and how do you manage encryption keys securely?

Answer: Encryption protects sensitive data during backup. I use built-in encryption features like FileVault and manage encryption keys securely, ensuring they are accessible only to authorized personnel.

5. How do you address the challenge of managing backups for macOS systems distributed across multiple locations or remote offices?

Answer: I may use a centralized backup solution with support for remote backups, leveraging technologies like VPNs or secure connections to ensure data from remote locations is backed up securely.

Advanced Topics:

1. Explain the role of snapshot-based backups in macOS, and how do they contribute to efficient backup and restore processes?

Answer: Snapshots capture the state of a file system at a specific point in time. They enable faster and more efficient backups by only recording changes since the last snapshot, reducing the backup window.

2. How do you integrate backup strategies with macOS Server features for centralized management and control?

Answer: macOS Server offers features like Time Machine Server, which allows centralized management of Time Machine backups. I would configure and manage these features based on organizational needs.

3. Can you discuss the considerations and challenges of implementing backup strategies for macOS systems in a virtualized environment?

Answer: Virtualized environments may require specialized backup solutions. I consider factors like integration with virtualization platforms, backup frequency, and data consistency during virtual machine snapshots.

4. In a scenario where a macOS system uses external RAID storage for critical data, how would you design a backup strategy to ensure data redundancy and quick recovery in case of a RAID failure?

Answer: I would implement regular backups of the RAID array, possibly using a combination of on-site and off-site solutions. Additionally, monitoring the health of the RAID array and addressing any issues promptly is crucial.

5. How would you approach the implementation of a disaster recovery plan for macOS systems, and what key components would you include?

Answer: A disaster recovery plan includes backup and restore procedures, off-site storage, documentation, and regular testing. I would ensure that all stakeholders are familiar with the plan and conduct periodic drills.

Troubleshooting and Maintenance:

1. How do you troubleshoot issues related to failed backups or errors in the backup logs on macOS?

Answer: I review backup logs for error messages, check system logs for relevant information, and use diagnostic tools like Console to identify and address issues affecting the backup process.

2. Explain the steps you would take to recover data from a corrupted backup file on macOS.

Answer: I would attempt to repair the backup file using tools provided by the backup solution. If unsuccessful, I might resort to extracting data from individual backup increments or seeking professional assistance.

3. In a scenario where a backup drive is lost or damaged, how would you address potential data loss and ensure continuity of operations?

Answer: I would rely on additional backup copies, potentially stored off-site or in the cloud. Regularly testing the restore process ensures that alternative backups are available in case of hardware failure.

4. How do you address issues related to backup storage running out of space, especially in environments with large and rapidly growing datasets?

Answer: I regularly monitor storage usage, adjust backup retention policies, and consider upgrading storage capacity as needed. Prioritizing and excluding non-essential data from backups can also help manage space effectively.

5. Can you provide an example of a challenging backup or restore issue you've encountered in your experience, and how you resolved it?

Answer: [Personalized response based on the candidate's experience.]

Emerging Trends and Technologies:

1. With the rise of edge computing and IoT devices, how do you envision adapting backup strategies for macOS systems to accommodate data generated at the edge?

Answer: Edge computing introduces challenges related to data volume and diversity. Adapting backup strategies involves considering distributed backup solutions and efficient data transfer methods.

2. How do you see artificial intelligence and machine learning influencing the field of backup and restore strategies for macOS in the future?

Answer: AI and ML could enhance predictive analytics for backup optimizations, automate data classification for efficient backups, and improve anomaly detection for early identification of potential issues.

3. As macOS evolves, what changes do you anticipate in backup and restore mechanisms, and how would you prepare for these changes?

Answer: I anticipate improvements in integration with cloud services, enhanced security features, and possibly more efficient backup formats. Staying informed and adapting backup strategies accordingly is crucial.

4. In a scenario where macOS introduces a new file system or storage technology, how would you approach migrating existing backup strategies to accommodate these changes?

Answer: I would thoroughly research and test the new technology, ensuring compatibility with existing backup solutions. Planning a phased migration and keeping abreast of vendor updates and recommendations would be key.

5. With the increasing reliance on cloud-based services, how would you adapt backup strategies for macOS to efficiently protect data stored in the cloud?

Answer: Adapting involves integrating with cloud backup services, understanding data residency and compliance requirements, and implementing a hybrid backup strategy to cover both on-premises and cloud-based data.

Monitoring and Performance Tuning

Monitoring:

1. What tools and utilities do you commonly use for monitoring system performance on macOS?

Answer: I use Activity Monitor, Console, top command in Terminal, and third-party tools like iStat Menus for real-time monitoring.

2. How do you identify and troubleshoot resource-intensive processes on a macOS system?

Answer: I analyze CPU, memory, and disk usage in Activity Monitor, use top for command-line insights, and check system logs for information on resource-hungry processes.

3. Explain the significance of system logs in monitoring macOS performance, and how do you extract meaningful information from them?

Answer: System logs contain valuable information about system events. I use Console to review logs, filter by relevant categories, and identify any issues affecting performance.

4. What role does the macOS Console app play in system monitoring, and how can it be utilized for troubleshooting?

Answer: Console consolidates system logs, making it easier to track issues. I use it to filter logs based on severity, timestamp, or specific processes, aiding in effective troubleshooting.

5. How do you monitor network activity on a macOS system, and what tools do you use to analyze network performance?

Answer: I use Activity Monitor for basic network monitoring and tools like Wireshark for in-depth analysis. Monitoring commands like nettop provide real-time insights into network usage.

6. Can you discuss the role of Energy and Memory tabs in Activity Monitor and how they contribute to system monitoring?

Answer: The Energy tab shows power usage, and the Memory tab details RAM usage. Both are crucial for monitoring system health and identifying resource-intensive applications.

7. How do you monitor disk I/O and identify potential bottlenecks on a macOS system?

Answer: I use Activity Monitor for a quick overview and tools like iostat or iotop in Terminal for detailed disk I/O monitoring. Elevated disk activity may indicate potential bottlenecks.

8. In a scenario where a macOS system is experiencing intermittent performance issues, how do you approach identifying and resolving the problem?

Answer: I start by reviewing system logs in Console, checking Activity Monitor for resource spikes, and using monitoring tools to identify patterns during performance degradation.

Performance Tuning:

1. What strategies do you employ to optimize CPU performance on a macOS system, especially during resource-intensive tasks?

Answer: I prioritize processes, adjust application settings, and use tools like Activity Monitor to identify and optimize CPU-intensive tasks. Terminal commands like nice and renice may be used.

2. How do you optimize memory usage on a macOS system to prevent slowdowns and improve overall performance?

Answer: I identify memory-hungry applications in Activity Monitor, manage startup items, and may use terminal commands like purge to free up inactive memory.

3. Discuss the role of macOS cache mechanisms in performance, and how do you manage caches for optimal system operation?

Answer: Caches improve system performance by storing frequently accessed data. I monitor cache sizes using Activity Monitor and may manually clear specific caches if necessary.

4. In a scenario where a macOS system exhibits slow boot times, how do you diagnose and address the issue?

Answer: I review startup items in System Preferences, use Activity Monitor to identify resource-intensive processes, and check system logs for errors during the boot process.

5. How do you optimize graphics performance on a macOS system, especially for tasks like video editing or graphic-intensive applications?

Answer: I update graphics drivers, adjust display settings, and may use third-party tools or Terminal commands to optimize GPU performance for specific applications.

6. Can you explain the impact of virtual memory on macOS performance, and how do you adjust virtual memory settings if needed?

Answer: Virtual memory allows the system to use disk space as additional RAM. I adjust virtual memory settings based on system requirements, considering factors like available disk space and usage patterns.

7. How do you optimize disk performance on macOS, and what steps do you take to prevent fragmentation?

Answer: I use tools like Disk Utility for disk maintenance, optimize file systems, and avoid near-full disk conditions. macOS, especially with APFS, handles fragmentation efficiently.

Resource Management:

1. Explain the concept of multitasking on macOS, and how do you manage system resources to ensure smooth multitasking performance?

Answer: Multitasking involves running multiple processes concurrently. I manage resources by monitoring CPU and memory usage, prioritizing tasks, and optimizing applications.

2. How do you optimize the startup process on a macOS system to reduce boot times and improve overall performance?

Answer: I manage startup items in System Preferences, disable unnecessary login items, and may use third-party tools to identify and control startup processes.

3. Discuss the impact of background processes and daemons on macOS performance, and how do you manage or disable them if necessary?

Answer: Background processes can consume resources. I use Activity Monitor and launchctl to identify and manage daemons, ensuring they align with system requirements.

4. How would you address a situation where a macOS system experiences overheating during resource-intensive tasks, affecting performance?

Answer: I would optimize cooling solutions, check for dust in hardware components, adjust system settings for fan control, and may use tools to monitor temperature and identify culprits.

5. In a macOS environment with multiple users, how do you ensure fair resource allocation and prevent one user from impacting the performance of others?

Answer: I manage user accounts, set resource limits where applicable, and use tools like renice to adjust process priorities for fair resource allocation.

macOS Integration:

1. How does macOS handle power management, and what strategies do you employ to optimize power consumption without sacrificing performance?

Answer: I leverage macOS power management features, adjust settings for energy efficiency, and may use third-party tools to fine-tune power consumption based on usage patterns.

2. Explain the role of macOS Spotlight in system performance, and how do you optimize indexing to balance search functionality and resource usage?

Answer: Spotlight indexes files for quick searches. I manage indexing preferences to exclude unnecessary locations and optimize indexing schedules for minimal impact on performance.

3. How do you integrate performance monitoring and tuning strategies with macOS security features like System Integrity Protection (SIP) and Gatekeeper?

Answer: I ensure that tuning strategies align with security policies. For example, I consider SIP restrictions when adjusting system files and ensure that Gatekeeper settings are compatible with application optimizations.

4. Discuss the impact of macOS updates on system performance, and how do you prepare for updates to minimize disruptions?

Answer: Updates may introduce performance improvements. I ensure backups are current, test updates in a controlled environment, and monitor post-update performance for any issues.

5. How do you optimize macOS systems for effective performance in a mixed environment with both Mac and Windows users?

Answer: I consider compatibility issues, optimize file-sharing settings, and may use tools like Parallels or Boot Camp for running Windows on Macs, ensuring a smooth coexistence.

Advanced Tuning Techniques:

1. In a macOS environment with SSD and HDD storage, how do you optimize performance and storage utilization using Fusion Drive or manual tiering?

Answer: I may use Fusion Drive for automated tiering or manually manage storage tiers based on usage patterns, ensuring frequently accessed data resides on the faster storage.

2. How would you approach tuning a macOS system for optimal performance in a virtualized environment?

Answer: I consider resource allocation, optimize virtual machine settings, and ensure seamless integration between the macOS host and virtualized environments for efficient performance.

3. Explain the process of optimizing network performance on a macOS system, especially in environments with high data transfer requirements.

Answer: I optimize network settings, may use Quality of Service (QoS) settings, and adjust parameters like TCP window size to ensure efficient and high-speed data transfers.

4. Can you discuss the considerations and challenges of performance tuning in macOS Server environments, and how it differs from individual systems?

Answer: In macOS Server environments, I focus on services, implement load balancing, optimize server settings, and ensure that performance enhancements align with the specific server roles.

5. How do you approach tuning a macOS system for optimal performance in creative industries, such as graphic design or video production?

Answer: I optimize GPU settings, allocate sufficient RAM for creative applications, and may customize system configurations to meet the demands of resource-intensive creative tasks.

Troubleshooting and Problem Resolution:

1. In a scenario where a macOS system exhibits intermittent performance issues, how do you approach identifying and resolving the problem?

Answer: I start by reviewing system logs in Console, checking Activity Monitor for resource spikes, and using monitoring tools to identify patterns during performance degradation.

2. How do you troubleshoot issues related to slow network performance on a macOS system, especially in environments with complex network configurations?

Answer: I use network monitoring tools, check for issues with routers or switches, inspect system logs for network-related errors, and may use packet capture tools for in-depth analysis.

3. Discuss the steps you would take to address a situation where a macOS system experiences frequent freezes or hangs, impacting user productivity.

Answer: I review system logs for error messages, check Activity Monitor for resource-intensive processes, and may use diagnostics tools to identify the root cause of the freezes.

4. How do you handle issues related to kernel panics on a macOS system, and what steps do you take to prevent recurrent panics?

Answer: I review panic logs for clues, check hardware components for issues, ensure drivers are up-to-date, and may disable or replace problematic kernel extensions.

5. Can you provide an example of a challenging monitoring or performance tuning issue you've encountered in your experience, and how you resolved it?

Answer: [Personalized response based on the candidate's experience.]

Future Trends and Technologies:

1. With the increasing use of Apple Silicon in Macs, how do you anticipate performance tuning strategies evolving for macOS systems with these processors?

Answer: Apple Silicon introduces new considerations. Tuning strategies may focus on optimizing applications for ARM architecture and leveraging the enhanced performance capabilities of Apple Silicon.

2. How do you envision artificial intelligence and machine learning impacting the field of monitoring and performance tuning for macOS in the future?

Answer: AI and ML could automate performance analysis, predict potential issues, and provide intelligent recommendations for tuning based on usage patterns and system behavior.

3. As macOS continues to integrate with cloud services, how do you foresee performance tuning strategies adapting to optimize cloud-based workflows and data storage?

Answer: Tuning strategies will likely involve optimizing for efficient data transfer, considering latency in cloud-based applications, and ensuring compatibility with cloud storage and processing solutions.

4. In a scenario where macOS introduces new performance-related features or technologies, how would you adapt existing tuning strategies to leverage these advancements?

Answer: I would stay informed about new features, test their impact on performance, and adjust tuning strategies to take advantage of any improvements or optimizations introduced by macOS.

5. With the evolution of macOS updates and features, how do you anticipate the role of monitoring and performance tuning changing in the coming years?

Answer: Monitoring and tuning will likely become more integrated with automation, providing proactive insights and recommendations. Continuous adaptation to new technologies and updates will remain crucial.

ONLINE RESOURCES

Practice Paper Link: https://forms.gle/cKp7FbBMBVBhnm9D9

QR Code:

Video Link: https://www.youtube.com/playlist?list=PLzlh_31VWEFpwtvDXXmDrP1NFZu34Qlne

QR Code:

ADDITIONAL RESOURCES

Linux Operating System Interview Questions and Answers Videos Playlist-

Link: https://www.youtube.com/playlist?list=PLzlh_31VWEFpihbhIZowbcatLKj0I10pF

QR Code:

YouTube Videos Playlists for all Chapters

CHAPTER 1 Link:https://www.youtube.com/playlist?list=PLzlh_31VWEFoRsAoogmEKdH0PSKSlA9c9

QR Code:

CHAPTER 2 Link:https://www.youtube.com/playlist?list=PLzlh_31VWEFqk6XUc8iCNB0vW2J4Y3CSA

QR Code:

CHAPTER 3 Link:https://www.youtube.com/playlist?list=PLzlh_31VWEFq0ImTAlVGf-YHXLZo-XI6d

QR Code:

CHAPTER 4 Link:https://www.youtube.com/playlist?list=PLzlh_31VWEFoCHKXDCKJ7c6vn8tefsfQN

QR Code:

CHAPTER 5 Link:https://www.youtube.com/playlist?list=PLzlh_31VWEFq9GyFdTzTdIQYw8Yh39CEF

QR Code:

CHAPTER 6 Link:https://www.youtube.com/playlist?list=PLzlh_31VWEFoz2P0J7n1-OkrkmdQuYJ_j

QR Code:

CHAPTER 7 Link:https://www.youtube.com/playlist?list=PLzlh_31VWEFpGBHf2btDfkIXVAf7ndV4c

QR Code:

CHAPTER 8 Link:https://www.youtube.com/playlist?list=PLzlh_31VWEFoy5NPlWesJulwbo6LTGwHq

QR Code:

CHAPTER 9 Link:https://www.youtube.com/playlist?list=PLzlh_31VWEFptNJTD-9dKfvCEdDU8Jxyd

QR Code:

CHAPTER 10 Link:https://www.youtube.com/playlist?list=PLzlh_31VWEFphKu-eJx1KnT18uETnLAGU

QR Code:

CHAPTER 11 Link:https://www.youtube.com/playlist?list=PLzlh_31VWEFo3cdjLQMQZUDtoK8RUlvkS

QR Code:

CHAPTER 12 Link:https://www.youtube.com/playlist?list=PLzlh_31VWEFpwtvDXXmDrP1NFZu34Qlne

QR Code:

mac OS Interview QUestions & Answers Liink:

https://www.youtube.com/playlist?list=PLzlh_31VWEFpihbhIZowbcatLKj0I10pF

QR Code: